C ONTENTS

Acknowledgements

Our first and greatest expression of gratitude must be to those staff and pupils in schools which participated in the LAPP evaluation study. Our sincere thanks are due to them for the way they accommodated our various requests, provided crucial information and insights, and were more than generous with their time, during a period which made greater than normal demands on people's professional expertise and commitment. We hope that they may stand to gain something, too, from their participation.

We should also like to thank our colleagues from the previous phase of the study - Brandon Ashworth, Orlinda Dias, John Harland, Kerry Giles, Clare Mangan, Jenny Mills, Nick Oatley and Monica Taylor - on whose assiduous data collection we have often depended.

The Handbook could not have seen the light of day without the patient fortitude of our secretary Lynn Fardell.

An especial debt of gratitude is due to the project leader, Penelope Weston, who has guided the research and evaluation process from its beginning through a time of unprecedented change in the national educational system. Penelope Weston has also contributed the final section on the role of the LEA in raising attainment. A full report on the LEAs in LAPP (*Investing in Reform: the long term implications for LEAs*) is available from the Department of Education and Science.

We should finally like to thank Sheila Stoney, the project director, and the members of the Steering Committee for their advice and support at crucial stages in the project.

DIFFERENTIATION IN ACTION

A WHOLE SCHOOL APPROACH FOR RAISING ATTAINMENT

by

ROBERT STRADLING

&

LESLEY SAUNDERS

with

PENELOPE WESTON

NATIONAL FOUNDATION
FOR EDUCATIONAL
RESEARCH, THE MERE
UPTON PARK, SLOUGH
BERKSHIRE, SL1 2DQ

LONDON HMSO
March 1991

ISBN 0 11 270733 5

How to Use This Handbook

The Handbook is organised to guide school planners through the sequence shown opposite.

It has also been designed to offer possibilities for teacher in-service training (INSET). Some further material for use on training days and other forms of school-based INSET can be found at the back of the Handbook.

THE CASE FOR DIFFERENTIATION

DIVERSITY OF PUPILS' LEARNING PROBLEMS

SECTION 1

IDENTIFICATION OF LEARNING NEEDS

POSSIBLE SOLUTIONS

SECTION 2

APPROPRIATE TYPES OF PROVISION

IMPLEMENTING CHANGE

SECTION 3

DILEMMAS IN MANAGING CHANGE

SECTION 4

WHOLE SCHOOL STRATEGIES FOR RAISING ATTAINMENT

SECTION 5

List of acronyms appearing in the text

BTEC	Business & Technician Education Council
CDT	Craft, Design and Technology
CGLI	City and Guilds of London Institute
CSE	Certificate of Secondary Education
DES	Department of Education and Science
ERA	Education Reform Act 1988
EWO	Education Welfare Officer
FE	Further Education
FTE	Full-Time Equivalent
GCE	General Certificate of Education
GCSE	General Certificate of Secondary Education
HoD	Head of Department
IE	Instrumental Enrichment
ILEA	Inner London Education Authority
INSET	In-Service Education and Training
IQ	Intelligence Quotient
LAPP	Lower Attaining Pupils Programme
LEA	Local Education Authority
LMS	Local Management of Schools
MPG	Main Professional Grade
NFER	National Foundation for Educational Research
PE	Physical Education
PSE	Personal and Social Education
PTR	Pupil:Teacher Ratio
RoA	Record of Achievement
RoSLA	Raising of the School Leaving Age
SAT	Standard Assessment Task
SEN	Special Educational Needs
SMT	Senior Management Team
TVEI	Technical and Vocational Education Initiative
YT	Youth Training

I NTRODUCTION:

ABOUT THIS HANDBOOK

The Origins of the Handbook

The Handbook has grown out of a five-year evaluation programme conducted by a team from the National Foundation for Educational Research (NFER) of initiatives funded to tackle the issue of effective provision for so-called lower attaining pupils in their last two years of compulsory schooling. During this period (1984-89) when such far-reaching changes were taking place both in the education system and in the debate about education, it became increasingly apparent that the original brief was too narrowly defined in terms of:

- **the age group** - pupils aged 14-16;

- **the definition of 'lower attaining'** - pupils for whom existing (pre-GCSE) examinations at 16+ had not been designed;

- **the agenda** - ensuring that more young people of this age group left school with skills and qualifications they could use.

The findings of the evaluation team, working with LEAs and schools over the whole of this challenging period, suggest that a more useful way of defining the task facing secondary schools might be:

- developing more effective **provision for all pupils,** appropriate to their diverse and changing needs.

The Handbook provides a way of using the evidence obtained from schools which took part in these initiatives funded under the umbrella of the Lower Attaining Pupils Programme (LAPP) in order to argue this case and to provide practical guidance for developing a whole school strategy for optimising the achievements of all pupils.

The argument and suggestions for action are throughout based on evidence from NFER's national evaluation of LAPP (see note below) and particularly its second phase (1988-89). Most of the evidence arises from case studies of a small number of schools, which we use to reveal - through vignettes of particular circumstances - the complexity of the processes at work, but only in order to suggest ways in which that complexity can be addressed outside the context of a funded programme. Large-scale changes in the educational world have impinged directly on, and with profound significance for, provision for low attainers in the secondary school: the most important of these are the implementation of GCSE (which raised afresh all the central questions about appropriate 14-16 curriculum, pedagogy and accreditation for all pupils) and the Education Reform Act 1988 (which offers challenges and opportunities to educationalists and the wider community on curricular, organisational and financial fronts simultaneously).

We envisage the Handbook being used to assist planning and review procedures and to support INSET sessions. We have learnt a great deal from the teachers and managers in the schools with whom we have been working and we are glad to acknowledge here the extent to which we have drawn on their collective insights and experience.

A Note on the Lower Attaining Pupils Programme

The programme was announced by Sir Keith Joseph, then Secretary of State for Education and Science, in July 1982 with the aim of funding experiments in improving the quality and effectiveness of 14-16 education for the range of pupils for whom existing examinations (GCE and GCSE) had not been initially designed. Finding ways of raising pupils' attainment and motivation in the last two years of compulsory schooling and of enabling them to be better prepared for adult and working life was central to the challenge confronting schools. A team from NFER was commissioned by the DES to evaluate the programme.

Seventeen LEA's mounted pilot projects and have been continuing the work of sustaining and disseminating the progress made, with the help of central funding, over the six years of the programme. The projects varied considerably in their educational, organisational and resourcing approaches; the task of the evaluation team has been to review the effectiveness of the programme as a whole and its implications for other LEAs and schools, while doing justice both to the diversity of the initiatives and to the complexity of issues they generated.

Previous reports on the programme by the NFER evaluation team are listed at the back of the Handbook.

THE CHALLENGE OF DIVERSITY: LOW ATTAINERS IN THE SECONDARY SCHOOL

THE DEBATE ON DIFFERENTIATION

Since its emergence in *Better Schools* (DES, 1986) as one of the four marks of the acceptable curriculum (broad, balanced, relevant and differentiated) differentiation has been a key issue in any consideration of the processes of curriculum change and planning.

Most teachers would probably accept that their pupils tend to learn in different ways and at different speeds, and that within any year group, and even within any class, there will be marked variations in the levels of attainment they achieve and the kinds of learning difficulties and problems they experience. There is likely to be far less agreement about how best to respond to this diversity. Some kind of 'differentiation' seems to be called for but it has become a loaded word associated with long-standing debates about comprehensive schooling and more recent ones concerning the National Curriculum. The dilemma articulated by HMI in 1980 is just as sharp today.

> 'The curriculum has to satisfy two seemingly contrary requirements. On the one hand it has to reflect the broad aims of education which hold good for all children, whatever their abilities and whatever the schools they attend. On the other hand it has to allow for difference in the abilities and other characteristics of children, even of the same age.'
> (HMI, *A View of Curriculum*, HMSO, 1980).

This leaves a number of important questions unanswered: can these differences be adequately met by grouping pupils according to ability or past performance? Does differentiation necessarily imply teaching different curricula to different pupils (whether in groups or individually)? Or, can differentiation be realised through teaching the same curriculum to all pupils but tailoring the teaching approaches and processes to the different learning needs of individual pupils?

Generally speaking, schools either opt for establishing a group of lower attaining pupils on a permanent or semi-permanent basis, either within subjects or across the curriculum, or they choose to differentiate through identifying the learning needs of individual pupils and attempting to tailor the provision accordingly. (For more details of the variety of forms of differentiation which actually emerged within LAPP as a whole see an earlier NFER Report *(Frameworks for Learning))*.

Of course these two broad strategies are not necessarily mutually exclusive. In some schools the procedures for grouping pupils are more flexible than in others allowing, for example, for re-grouping for different purposes. Procedures for differentiating between individuals *within* groups of lower attainers were also apparent in some schools. Nevertheless, it was possible to detect differences between project schools in the degree of emphasis they gave to various forms of differentiation and this tendency is expressed graphically in **Diagram 1.**

Schools which emphasise the need to differentiate between individual learners are more likely to be concerned that the broad, basic **goals of education** should

Diagram 1

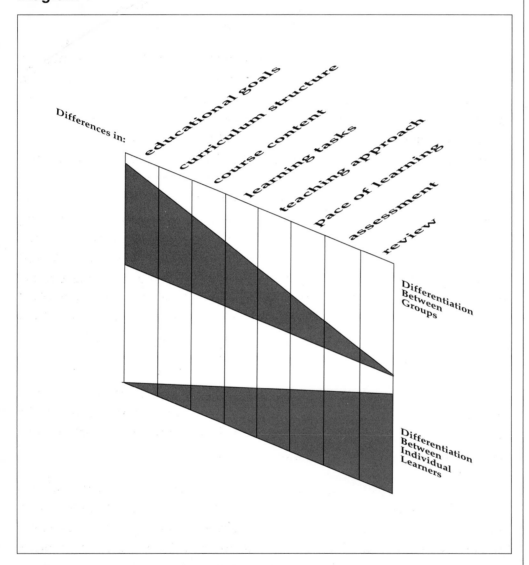

apply to all pupils across the ability range; that provision for lower attainers should be made within the existing **curriculum structure** (common core, options schemes, timetabling arrangements) or that the structure should be changed for all pupils (for example, by a shift to a modular curriculum or by extending the core curriculum and reducing the range of options). Similarly, **course content** tends to be substantially the same for all pupils, but with opportunities to take more practical and pre-vocational options. Alternatively, the basic curriculum may be 'enriched' by the provision of additional courses in 'thinking skills' and 'problem-solving', or cross-curricular initiatives such as the Wiltshire Oracy

Project. However, the commonest characteristics of differentiation between individual learners tend to be an emphasis on dialogue - in the form of a regular **review** - between teachers and individual pupils about their progress and their learning needs, based on formative and diagnostic **assessment.** The **pace of learning** is often negotiable, or teachers provide **learning tasks** and activities which are flexible enough to adjust to the learning speed of each pupil (e.g. projects and modules). This in turn often necessitates changes in **teaching approaches** towards more pupil-centred learning activities.

By contrast, schools which can be located towards the other end of the differentiation spectrum (because they put much more emphasis on differentiation between groups of pupils) seem less certain about whether the same basic **goals of education** should apply to all pupils across the ability range. Some, for example, express misgivings about the relevance of breadth and balance to the curriculum diet of lower attainers. Indeed, some argue that by building breadth and balance into provision for this target group they could be driving some 14-16 year olds away from school. Allowing pupils to specialise in a few activities where they achieve some success is often held to be a more effective strategy for improving attendance and motivation. This point of view often goes hand-in-hand with the provision of a **different curriculum structure** through, for example, a blocked timetable or a 'primary school approach' (where pupils spend a considerable part of each week with the same teacher), and the provision of different kinds of **course content** from that which prevails in the mainstream curriculum. (For a discussion of different kinds of course provision, see Section 3 ADDRESSING THE DIVERSITY.)

The greatest area of overlap between these two types of differentiation lies in changes in **teaching approach**. Many schools stress the importance of this for raising attainment, but in practice the extent to which changes in teaching style and pedagogy actually occur is highly variable.

It should be stressed that Diagram 1 represents two broad trends within schools as a whole about how best to respond to the needs of lower attaining pupils. These are ideal types and you can often find elements of both approaches within the same school. It is possible, for example, to find schools which differentiate between groups and then differentiate between individual learners within the lower attainers' group. Others differentiate between individuals in some areas of the curriculum and between groups in other areas.

> The purpose behind the diagram and the accompanying discussion is to draw attention to the various elements of differentiation and the kinds of issues which need to be considered when planning to introduce a new initiative to improve the performance of some or all pupils within the school.

THE PUPILS

The target group for LAPP, as for so many other initiatives, was the 'early leavers' and, in particular, the so-called 'bottom forty per cent'. But as has been argued in recent NFER reports, amongst others, the age of 14 is too late to address the task of raising the attainment of this target group. Later in the Handbook we suggest that initiatives at 14 often tend to be 'holding devices' for coping with an identifiable group of 'difficult' pupils rather than solutions to the problem of lower attainment. Nevertheless, it would be naive not to recognise that in many schools the problems of low attendance rates, lack of motivation, disruptive or withdrawn behaviour, poor basic skills and learning skills, and failure in conventionally academic terms within the fourth and fifth year are extensive, urgent and impossible to ignore. The imperative of responding to such problems in an effective way in the short term still needs to be an integral part of any longer term strategy for raising attainment throughout the whole school.

Schools usually have little difficulty in accepting that some pupils in the 14-16 age range are failing to meet conventional expectations of educational adequacy and that there are shortcomings in the educational system which contribute to this. The difficulties arise when it comes to identifying individual pupils' learning needs and problems and responding to them in appropriate ways. As we have already pointed out, many schools choose to identify a group with apparently common needs and provide them with a partially or wholly differentiated curriculum.

In reality, however, the pupils identified as low attainers turn out to be a highly diverse population. To give some idea of the extent of this diversity, we have produced on the following pages six thumbnail sketches of pupils taken at random from different schools. You can see that they all have very different needs and problems and yet they have all been labelled (formally or informally) by their respective schools as 'lower attainers'. The fact that four of the six pupils are boys is no accident. In many schools where a group of lower attainers is identified there tends to be a bias in favour of boys, reflecting the fact that selection criteria are implicit as well as explicit. Attainment or academic performance might be the explicit criterion for selection, but a history of disruptive behaviour is often an additional, though unstated, factor behind the selection process.

> **Schools usually have little difficulty in accepting that some pupils in the 14-16 age range are failing to meet conventional expectations.**
>
> **The difficulties arise when it comes to identifying individual pupils' learning needs and problems and responding to them in appropriate ways.**

Kevin
Fifteen years of age, living with his grandmother because of a history of child abuse at home. Tall for his age. Reports from primary school indicated that he was bright. His work seemed to be alright until the end of the second year at his secondary school, then he started playing truant a lot. He was nominated for the LAPP project by six different teachers at the end of the third year mainly because of his poor attendance and low motivation.

Andy

Nearly sixteen; a burly, good-humoured lad. Sometimes absent from school with migraine. An easy-going attitude to life and work, comes to school to meet his mates. From his first year at the secondary school, his reports have said: 'If Andy stopped playing the clown, he would achieve a lot more'. Has shown some potential in maths and French but is not doing GCSE in either. Tries to do the bare minimum and mostly succeeds. Is regarded by some of his teachers as a bit disruptive. Wants to go on a vocational training course at the local FE college. Favourite hobby: watching television.

We have found the term 'lower attainer' being used to refer to:

- **pupils with special educational needs,** whether on the grounds of cognitive ability or of sensory disability;

- **pupils with persistent learning problems,** often first identified in primary school and re-identified periodically;

- **pupils with an ingrained sense of failure:** those who would rather drop out than take exams or tests;

- **pupils who seem to be coping well until puberty:** for some, at least, the onset of pubic hair, acne, sex and the humiliations of the changing room become more important than doing well in geography or chemistry;

- **pupils performing poorly across the whole curriculum** by comparison with their peers;

- **pupils having difficulties only with some subjects;**

- **pupils having problems with one or more basic skills,** which may or may not be having a deleterious effect on their school work in general;

- **pupils convinced that the curriculum is irrelevant:** the ones who come to school to meet their mates and expect to go on to YT at sixteen;

- **habitual truants:** by no means always the least able;

- **pupils who attend every lesson in body but seldom in mind or spirit;**

- **pupils who seem to be progressing reasonably well until emotionally swamped with problems at home.**

This range of learning needs and difficulties and the behavioural and motivational problems associated with them are reflected in the changes in thinking and the organisational changes brought about since the Warnock Report (DES, 1978) and the 1981 Education Act. In particular they reflect the post-Warnock view that any child, of any level of ability, from any background, can at some time have some special educational needs that have to be met within mainstream education.

In response to this diversity of learning needs and problems schools often polarise into two camps: those who perceive the problem as **'pupils failing school'** and those who perceive it as **'school failing pupils'**. As you can see from **Diagram 2,** the left-hand column depicts what is essentially a 'deficit model' of low attainment: the child is failing because of his or her poor grasp of fundamental skills and processes, or through lack of self-motivation, or through factors in her or his background, or some combination of all three. The right-hand column, by contrast, starts from the premise that the school is not doing enough to identify the learning needs and difficulties of its pupils and to respond adequately to them. Stereotypical assumptions perhaps, but they often determine how a school responds to the perceived problem of lower attainment.

Diagram 2

Polarised assumptions about the problem of lower attainment

'Pupils failing school'	'School failing pupils'
poor basic skills	inadequate diagnosis of need
poor personal and social skills	irrelevant curriculum content
poor attendance and behaviour	inappropriate pedagogy
poor motivation and self image	low expectation (by teachers)
low parental expectations	unfavourable PTR
social deprivation	lax discipline
poor parental support	non-conducive environment

Just as there are a number of quite different needs and problems associated with lower attaining pupils, so schools also experience and define these problems according to a number of different institutional constraints (discussed on pages 47-49) and characteristics. Moreover, specific local differences mean that approaches which work in one school cannot be assumed to work in another, even when both schools share similar internal characteristics and priorities.

The eight schools described briefly on the following pages illustrate a fairly representative range. We shall return throughout this Handbook to these particular schools (fictitious in name but based on actual case study schools) to show how different contexts and circumstances, different management strategies and different perceptions of the nature, scale and diversity of lower attainment within these schools have given rise to different 'solutions' and strategies and significantly influenced their implementation, institutionalisation and long-term impact. Four of these schools, **Bankside, Broomhill, Green Lane** and **Fairacre,** are dealt with in some detail throughout the Handbook in order to give a realistic sense of how and why things happened as they did. Material on the other four schools, **Robinswood, City Road, The King's** and **Little Stoke,** is

Sandra

Tall and heavily built. Hates games and PE. Lives with her mum, never knew her dad. The oldest of four, she usually gets kept at home to look after her youngest brother when her mother is ill - which happens quite frequently. Sandra suffers quite a bit of racial prejudice and harassment from her peers and usually responds violently. This has happened so often that she is beginning to lose the sympathy of some of the staff, who tend to see her as a trouble maker. Quite good at maths, science and art, where she tries hard; but she hates reading aloud or writing and gets upset when asked to do either. Before being nominated for the project, she tended to sit on her own and rarely participated.

Neil
Nearly sixteen, but a little immature. A speech impediment, for which he is receiving therapy. Adopted. Polite and eager to please, which manifests itself in trying hard: his pre-project school reports tended to be full of praise for his efforts if not his achieve-ments. At one time inclined to slightly bizarre forms of attention-seeking, which he seems to have grown out of. Not very fond of reading and writing; good relationships with his peers and regarded by his teachers as a rather voluble member of the group, with an engaging sense of humour. Wants to be a warehouseman.

intended to provide concise illustration of particular points. In addition, one other school, **Tweedmill**, appears once or twice because the innovations they are instituting appear to address the needs of all pupils in each year group, although it is too soon to make judgements about their relative success.

The wide-ranging differences to be found in these eight case study schools can be typified more generally in terms of the following factors:

- **Size:** ranging from two-form entry to ten-form entry schools.

- **Location:** ranging from three schools in inner city areas in the North to a school serving farming communities in a Shire county, two large suburban campus schools and two small-town schools in the South West and East Midlands.

- **Catchment area:** varying from multi-ethnic to predominantly white working class to catchment areas which represent a complete cross-section of society; from schools with relatively static catchment areas to those with constantly shifting populations.

- **Socio-economic context:** the North-South divide is still a factor. The northern-based case study schools were more likely to serve communities experiencing long-term unemployment and widespread social disadvantage brought about by the structural decline of local industries. By comparison, and even in the mid-1980s, the case study schools in the south of England tended to enjoy a situation where most school leavers, including low attainers, were able to go straight into paid employment.

- **Ability range:** varying from so-called 'sink schools' at one extreme to those where the ability levels of the school population approximate a normal distribution curve.

- **Age range:** including upper schools (13-16 or 13-18), 11-16 high schools and secondary schools catering for the full 11-18 age range, each of which seemed to experience different problems, especially in relation to provision for their lower attaining pupils.

- **History and tradition:** whilst some are 1960s purpose-built comprehensives, others are former secondary moderns or amalgamations of two secondary moderns, and one is an ex-grammar school.

- **Staffing:** falling pupil rolls mean that most of the case study schools have enjoyed favourable staffing ratios. This may temporarily have enabled them to opt for strategies such as individualised learning, in-class support teaching, team teaching and staff development through secondments as well as permitting curriculum planning and review meetings to be timetabled.

- **School organisation:** ranging from those schools with traditional and relatively autonomous departmental structures (schools with 20 or more departments) to those with a small number of faculties and even ones where most key curricular decisions are being taken by cross-curricular teams. They also vary from schools still operating a 40 period week to those where a great deal of flexibility has been provided through blocked timetabling.

- **Staff teams:** varying from schools where as few as two or three teachers were and are actively involved in provision for low attainers to those involving all teachers concerned with the fourth and fifth year curriculum and even some where virtually the entire staff participate in provision.

- **Selected or identified pupils:** ranging from less than ten per cent to whole year groups.

We have dwelt on this diversity in order to highlight four key points which should be kept in mind when planning provision for lower attainers:

- In the absence of universally accepted criteria for determining who are the 'lower attainers', most schools define them in relation to the distribution of attainment amongst the school's overall pupil intake. In other words, **'the lower attainer' is a relative concept.**

- Due to **organisational factors and constraints** most schools will not necessarily make provision for the educational needs of all their lower attainers but only those to which they think they can realistically respond. Most schools make special provision for about 10-12 per cent of the fourth and fifth years, even when by other criteria (e.g. pupil profiles, school records, NFER tests) they might be expected to respond to and cater for the learning needs and difficulties of a much larger group.

- Concepts such as 'lower attainer', 'low achiever' and 'slow learner' tend, as we have already seen, to be catch-all terms applied to often highly heterogeneous types of learners. As a result the concept tends to be far more arbitrarily applied than concepts more usually associated with SEN provision. As a result organisational criteria often play a more significant role in identifying 'lower attainers' than the individual learning needs and problems of the pupils selected.

- It is extremely difficult for any school to identify a group of 'lower attainers' with common needs and learning difficulties that can be responded to in a uniform way, but, again for organisational reasons, they will often be treated as if this was non-problematic.

This is why in subsequent sections of the Handbook we have preferred to focus on the problems of low attainment (and later, the problems of raising attainment for all) rather than the problem of the lower attainers.

Liam
Fourteen, small for his age and looks undernourished. Stable home life and a good attender. Bright as a button. Liam finishes his science experiments long before everyone else, so is inclined to invent his own experiments or play with the taps on the bunsen burner. Non-stop chatterbox with a very low threshold of boredom, which he takes no trouble to conceal. Much complained about by his teachers for the disruptive effect he has on their lessons, which may explain why he was nominated by a surprisingly large number of teachers for the LAPP project.

Sharon

Nearly sixteen, mature for her age; an only child. Stylish, wears make up and makes even the school uniform look fashionable. A veneer of self-assurance socially, but seems to lack confidence in her work. Tends to go around with a small tight-knit group of girl-friends who are mutually supportive, but are also diffident in lessons and tend to keep a low profile. Her main criticism of teachers is that 'they don't explain things properly'. Regarded by some teachers as poorly motivated. Doing seven GCSEs, but not expected to do very well in any of them. Tends to be allocated to the bottom sets. Plans to go to college to study beauty therapy, hairdressing and business studies. Wants to set up her own hairdressing salon.

THE SCHOOLS

Bankside School is a four-form entry school situated in an industrial estate close to the centre of a large northern city. Throughout the 1980s the school's catchment area experienced high levels of unemployment, and there is much social deprivation. Many of the pupils come from one-parent families and in 1986 just under half were receiving free school meals. On NFER Cognitive Ability tests approximately 75 per cent of Bankside's pupils achieved below average or average results when compared with national standards, and the school has a relatively high proportion of statemented children in each year. Staff feel that open enrolment is increasingly pushing the school towards becoming a 'sink school' for the inner city area. In 1986 the relatively new head decided that LAPP funding should be directed towards the problems of low attainment in the third year where the curriculum was highly traditional and compartmentalized into discrete subjects. The fourth and fifth year curriculum had already been overhauled to make it more practical and relevant to those unlikely to get any good passes at GCSE. It was now felt that the third year curriculum needed to be brought into line with this earlier development, ultimately by making the whole curriculum more integrated, more practical, and with more emphasis on cross-curricular skills and topics. In 1986-87 the reconstructed curriculum was offered to half the year group. In 1988-89 it was offered to all but a 'fast stream' of the 15 most able pupils.

Broomhill High School is a five-form entry school created in the late 1960s as a result of the amalgamation of two secondary moderns into one comprehensive. Throughout the 1980s it has experienced falling rolls: it was an eight-form entry school until 1984. The staff FTE has also been falling during the same period, in part as a response to falling rolls but also due to severe financial stringencies within the LEA. The school is situated near the inner ring road of a large northern conurbation. Most of the children live on council estates or in pre-war terraced housing. The area has experienced relatively high levels of unemployment during the '80s and most of the school leavers have gone on either to YT or to unskilled jobs. The school's GCSE results would not be regarded as good by any absolute national standards, but they compare reasonably well with other schools located in similar catchment areas with similar ranges of ability amongst the intake. In 1983 it was decided to provide an alternative curriculum, with heavy emphasis on active and experiential learning and 5-6 week modules, to one-third of the fourth and fifth year pupils. Selected pupils spent up to half the week in the same tutor group with one teacher to give them a greater sense of security and confidence.

Green Lane School is an upper school (13-19) of around 750 pupils situated near the centre of a thriving old town which has a relatively low rate of unemployment. Formerly a grammar school, it has some of the traditions and staff from those days, though in recent years has had a higher than average intake of lower ability pupils. This is thought by staff to be partly due to the reputation the school has established for its pastoral system. An increasing number of pupils (currently 13 per cent) come from ethnic minorities, notably Bangladeshi, and the school has two section XI teachers. Individual pupils from local special schools attend the school for part of their curriculum. Provision for around 25 pupils per year has been offered through LAPP, taking the form of a two year pre-vocational preparation course based on multi-agency provision, for fourth and fifth year pupils for whom GCSE courses are thought to be unsuitable. The 'project' is housed in a newly refurbished part of the school and maintains a separate ethos from the mainstream, enabling an informal and personal style of relationship between staff and students to predominate. However, falling pupil rolls and school reorganisation are resulting in cuts in staff numbers and a shift from the 'alternative curriculum' framework to a more diffuse provision for a larger number of pupils through special needs and support provision on an inter-faculty basis co-ordinated by the teacher who has previously been in charge of the LAPP pre-vocational course. This has been accompanied by a discernible change in the overt 'philosophy' of the school towards greater integration and liaison.

Fairacre School is a suburban school of around 700 pupils situated in the middle of a large housing estate (local authority and private) on the outskirts of a new town, though the school draws pupils from all over town. The school's intake is now increasing; the county is experiencing severely reduced pupil rolls (resulting in a number of school closures and mergers), but the school's growing reputation is countering this general trend. It used to have a higher than average intake of pupils with special needs; it was not a generally popular choice with parents. Since the advent of a new head a few years ago, however, the school has maintained its reputation for coping well with non-academic and disaffected pupils while building up its overall image to the point where this year's first year represents the highest number of first choice pupils in the area. Middle class parents with academic aspirations for their children are forming a larger group within the school than previously. Employment prospects in the area are good, with a high proportion of retail openings, and employers are in competition with each other for school leavers. Provision for low ability and under-achieving fourth and fifth year pupils takes the form of subject-based courses which carry a county certificate of achievement endorsed by one of the examining boards. Every pupil in theory can therefore undertake a programme of study suited to her or his individual abilities, composed of accredited subjects whether through GCSE or county scheme.

Robinswood High School is an eight-form entry 11-18 comprehensive created in 1970 by an amalgamation of a grammar and a secondary modern. It is situated on the outskirts of a medium-sized industrial town in the East Midlands. The main sources of employment in the locality are coal-mining, agriculture and light industry. Unemployment in the 1980s has been fairly high, especially for school leavers. The catchment area is socially polarized. Over three-quarters of the pupils come from localities designated by the local authority as 'severely disadvantaged' whilst 15 per cent live in one of the 'most advantaged' areas within the LEA. On NFER tests up to 40 per cent of pupils score below 90, and a significant proportion of them exhibit serious behavioural problems. In 1977 the school set up a separate unit for those with most severe problems of social adjustment. From the onset of LAPP in 1983 the school based its approach on the premiss that low attaining pupils are not a homogeneous target group, but represent a spectrum of pupils with varying learning needs and achievements. They rejected a discrete curriculum for low attainers and opted instead to retain a common, subject-based curriculum, but introduce cross-curricular skills and active learning strategies.

City Road Comprehensive is a two-form entry inner city 12-16 comprehensive with a total roll of 350, serving a predominantly white, working-class community. About 8 per cent of the school population are from ethnic minorities - Asian and Caribbean. Ninety five per cent of pupils come from ageing council estates in an area which has experienced high levels of unemployment since the mid-70s due mainly to the structural decline of the heavy industries which had long been the major source of employment in the town. There is widespread social deprivation, and this is reflected amongst pupils in terms of behavioural problems, poor attendance, apathy, low expectations and widespread underachievement. Due to falling rolls the school has continued to exist throughout the '80s under the threat first of amalgamation and then of closure. The school did not want to identify a specific group of 'LAPP pupils'. Instead they opted for a whole school approach. LAPP resources were directed towards staff development, an extended common curriculum with more modular courses and fewer options, and a greater emphasis on practical and skills-based learning. More recently it has started to tackle the problems of transition from primary to secondary by reducing the number of teachers with which each first year group comes into contact.

The King's School is a small school of 500 pupils situated in a rural area, which makes internal communication and the recognition and take-up of good practice relatively easy. Apart from statemented pupils and those with learning difficulties, the school has a number of travellers' children on its register. The school has changed substantially with the appointment of a new head. There used to be a conventional remedial menu for lower ability pupils, supplemented in the upper school by a vocational skills course through the local FE college. The policy of the school is now 'to enable every child to reach his or her potential' which is to be realized through organisational and structural as well as curricular means. Thus the policy has recently been embodied in the form of a new appointment, a post which has oversight of all forms of pupil support, including responding to self-referral by pupils, liaison with outside bodies and co-ordinating support teaching. The member of staff also undertakes internal INSET and awareness-raising amongst staff on the issues of giving pupils equal access to all aspects of the curriculum. Provision for lower attaining pupils in the fourth and fifth year has been supplemented by a 'foundation course', newly instituted this year. Sensitivity to the travellers' culture - which has historically been oral rather than literate and therefore may suggest different teaching and learning strategies in schools - is clearly crucial. There is also, of course, a tradition of mobility which, in an education system based on settled urban and industrial ways of life, poses problems of regular attendance. Liaison with outside agencies like the Education Welfare Officer (EWO) also plays a central role in ensuring that such pupils get the most out of their schooling. The school is likely to receive some extra assistance for small schools under LMS, which it badly needs if - for example - progress in materials and profiling development is not to be impeded for lack of photocopying funds.

Little Stoke is a large school in a small rural town, but its proximity to the rapidly expanding conurbation which provides much of the employment in the area (a high proportion of micro-electronics and associated industries) means that it does not conform to the typical notion of a rural school. A sizeable proportion of the population commutes to the large town; many parents are likely to be 'upwardly mobile' and looking for an academic and technical education for their children. It is also the only school in the area with a sixth form. It has a good academic record and a low turnover of staff; at the moment, pupil rolls are falling (from ten form entry down to eight) and numbers will trough at around 1,150 in 1993. There will be little local competition under open enrolment, though: each town tends to have one state secondary school. It was, therefore, none of the obvious factors which propelled the school towards funded project provision. Rather, it was the opinion of local employers that many school leavers were insufficiently articulate and rather passive which encouraged the school to become involved in the LEA project some five years after it had been initiated. Although this was part of LAPP, the school did not target just the lower attaining pupils for oracy work. A small group of volunteer teachers from five departments have developed different approaches to oracy. Six departments are now fully involved. In practice, there is a wide range of interpretation of oracy at both curricular and organisational levels - for example, as group and individual 'talk', as active learning/role play, or as a tool for encouraging cross-curricular and inter-departmental liaison. There is a corresponding difficulty about 'mapping' what oracy work is being done, and *a fortiori* about how effective it is at raising confidence and/or attainment. But these issues are starting to be addressed, primarily through action research by teachers.

T

H E

CHALLENGE

O F

DIVERSITY:

PROBLEMS

AND

ATTEMPTED

SOLUTIONS

ANALYSING 'LOW ATTAINMENT'

The ongoing requirement for schools to organise and implement provision (e.g. for pupils who will not be taking GCSEs next year or for a group of youngsters who are disrupting every class they attend) has an institutional momentum which usually outstrips the need for discussion about the general problem of lower attainment or the specific learning needs and problems of a particular group. If discussion and review take place, they are often informal and *ad hoc* between like-minded staff and find characteristic expression in innovative, but often individual changes of practice. It is usually only when the school already has other, stronger incentives for review and change (such as new personnel in the school's senior management team, the introduction of GCSE, the need to plan for the National Curriculum and testing or changes in the pupil intake brought about by falling rolls and open enrolment), that they begin to respond to this more general, longer-term problem of lower attainment.

Boxes 1-4 form a sequence which takes us through the following stages of analysis: typology of lower attainment (Box 1), typical characteristics (Box 2), contributory factors (Box 3) and possible solutions (Box 4).

The types of lower attainment listed in **Box 1:**

❑ long-term low attainment

❑ short-term learning problems

❑ subject-specific learning difficulties

❑ consistent underachievement

❑ reluctance to learn

thus form the basis for subsequently analysing characteristics, contributory factors and solutions.

In **Box 1** we have set out the main **categories of lower attainment** which emerged from discussion with staff in case study LEAs and schools. It is worth reiterating at this point that this typology classifies not different types of lower attainer but different manifestations of lower attainment in individual pupils.

The purpose of this classification is to aid the process of:

• identifying different kinds of learning needs;

• relating the problem to possible contributory factors; and then

• identifying possible responses or 'solutions' which might be adopted singly or as part of a package.

In using this box four points need to be kept in mind:

- The problem of lower attainment is not always perceived by teaching staff as: 'what are the causes of lower attainment and when and how should they be tackled?' but rather 'what are we going to do with those young people who are going to opt out, fail or perform poorly in GCSE?' In other words, the issue is interpreted as one of determining how best to contain the problem of lower attainers rather than how best to tackle the problem of lower attainment.

- During the 1980s we have seen established ideas about attainment challenged from within and outside schools. Broader and more demanding definitions have emerged extending attainment well beyond the absorption and presentation of knowledge to include the practical applications of skills, concepts and knowledge, problem-solving, personal and social skills and even personal qualities. This has also led to new thinking about how best to assess and record these broader forms of attainment through the introduction of oral assessment, profiling and records of achievement. Yet at the same time there have been other pressures in schools to restore more traditional definitions of attainment which are likely to reinforce the sense of failure of many children.

- Any discussion of a concept such as 'lower attainment' must ultimately confront the question 'lower than what?' Very often it is assumed that the answer is 'lower than the rest of the age group', although it could also be 'lower than the pupil's potential indicates' and 'lower than the required standard for a given course'.

- While we want to insist on the propriety of making a distinction between lower attainers and lower attainment, we have found - even in our own research discussions - a 'slippage' between these concepts. But, in the end, we are talking about real pupils and how best to help them. So we acknowledge that the distinction is an ideal to be aimed at in trying to clarify the issues, rather than a rubric which can be readily applied.

The categories in **Box 1** are broad, and each tends to embrace a number of distinct learning needs and difficulties or characteristics of the problem. These are outlined in **Box 2**. Taken separately they may be symptomatic of more than one kind of problem, and whilst some learners may exhibit all the characteristics of one category of problem there is no reason why this should necessarily be the case.

Box 2 is intended to draw attention to the widespread tendency to encompass within the broad yet relative term 'lower attainment' not just the problems associated with poor basic skills (low scores on verbal and non-verbal cognitive

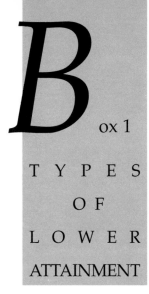

Long-term low attainment

Long-term widespread low attainment across the curriculum, usually coupled with low scores on cognitive ability tests and reading tests.

Short-term learning problems

Short-term learning problems in some or all areas of the curriculum; applies to pupils going through a 'difficult patch' and needing immediate but temporary additional help and support.

Subject-specific learning difficulties

Specific learning difficulties in a particular subject or skill area, especially in those parts of the curriculum (e.g. mathematics and languages) where learning is essentially cumulative and sequential, and where significant gaps in learning tend to have an adverse effect on subsequent developments.

Consistent underachievement

Past records in primary and secondary schools indicative of a problem of consistent underachievement, i.e. a widening gap between a pupil's potential and her or his performance in some or all areas of the curriculum, whether that gap be measured in terms of IQ and cognitive ability tests or in terms of subjective judgements by teachers.

Reluctance to learn

In the absence of severe or even moderate learning difficulties, little or no progress or signs of application.

Each of the above headings is given a column in Boxes 2, 3 and 4.

functioning tests and reading ages two - three years behind the average) but also those learning needs and difficulties which, for a variety of reasons, can emerge at any time and are amenable to short-term remediation. Of the other three categories, one of the most commonly represented is reluctance to learn, especially among the 14-16 age group: those who have 'switched off' or are highly selective in their attendance and participation. Those schools particularly concerned with reorganising or supplementing their ability to deliver the whole of the National Curriculum tend to be preoccupied with subject-specific learning difficulties and with underachievement by the average and above-average learner.

Regardless of which kinds of problem may predominate in a school, if those responsible for planning provision are to direct resources effectively to tackling the problems of lower attainment, they will need to identify the types, the range and the extent of the learning needs and difficulties of all pupils and not assume that pupils in a particular band, set or other similar grouping necessarily share the same needs and problems.

ATTEMPTING SOLUTIONS

Whether we are talking about the 20 per cent of pupils identified by Warnock or the 40 per cent identified by Sir Keith Joseph when launching LAPP, it would be fair to say that in most schools senior staff recognise that there is a sizeable number of 'low attainers' with diverse educational and social needs. But recognition of this diversity does not necessarily guide either the way schools target and select pupils for provision or even the kinds of teaching and learning strategies or curriculum provision they introduce. Sometimes it proves more convenient simply to take the bottom band and offer them an alternative curriculum; or to ignore the records compiled on pupils over the years by special needs staff and heads of year and instead take a straw poll in the staff-room (a good opportunity for some staff to off-load their more disruptive pupils); or to make provision for the lowest common denominator (e.g. 'they are all de-motivated so the best thing we can do is give them a course which they will find more relevant and less threatening than the mainstream curriculum'). Certainly in many schools there is little attempt to diagnose the learning needs of their target populations. Instead, the shape which each school's 'solution' takes often owes more to the influence of a number of constraints operating within each school - internal factors - as well as external factors beyond the control of the school.

> If those responsible for planning provision are to direct resources effectively to tackling the problems of lower attainment, they will need to identify the types, the range and the extent of the learning needs and difficulties of all pupils.

B ox 2

TYPICAL CHARACTER-ISTICS

	Long-term low attainment	Short-term learning problems	Subject- or skill-specific learning difficulties	Consistent underachievement	Reluctance to learn
poorly developed basic skills	✓		✓		
persistent below average scores on verbal and non-verbal cognitive functioning tests	✓				
difficulties in 'transferring' skills and knowledge	✓	✓	✓		
inability to learn from mistakes	✓				
poor study skills	✓	✓	✓	✓	
non-completion of assignments	✓	✓	✓	✓	✓
poor concentration and short attention span	✓		✓		
short memory span	✓				
lack of persistence and expectation of failure when attempting new tasks	✓		✓	✓	✓
high level of dependency on sympathetic teachers (needing constant attention, direction, supervision and reassurance)	✓				✓
poor capacity for self-expression	✓				
poor personal and social skills	✓				
low self-esteem and confidence	✓				
signs of anxiety, frustration and defensive behaviour	✓	✓			✓
disruptive or withdrawn behaviour	✓	✓		✓	✓
sudden deterioration in performance, attainment and organisation of work		✓	✓	✓	
starts to miss deadlines		✓	✓		
sudden decline in confidence and self-esteem		✓	✓	✓	
inconsistencies in performance and attitude depending on the task or the skills and understanding required	✓	✓	✓		
avoidance of tasks calling for certain skills, knowledge or procedures	✓	✓			
difficulties in comprehending certain concepts	✓	✓	✓		
difficulties with certain processes, operations and skills	✓		✓		
difficulties with the sequential learning structure of some subjects, e.g. maths, modern languages	✓		✓		
difficulties in interpreting abstractions	✓		✓		
difficulties with any kind of spatial representation	✓		✓		
problems with symbolic representation of knowledge	✓		✓		
difficulties in interpreting what is required of them in certain kinds of tasks	✓	✓	✓		
mismatch between classroom performance and potential as indicated by cognitive functioning tests, primary school reports etc.				✓	
inconsistent or erratic performance				✓	
apathetic non-participation in the classroom	✓				✓
non-attendance and poor attendance	✓				✓
frequent expression of view that school is boring and irrelevant	✓				✓

Internal Factors (a more detailed discussion of the internal factors appears in Section 4)

- ingrained assumptions and practices about the ability range of the pupil intake and how best to group them; about the 'causes' of lower attainment and about how best to respond to their needs;

- pragmatic adjustments to the school's organisational priorities to make the innovation conform to established arrangements;

- limited procedures for identifying learning needs and problems;

- the pressure to demonstrate a tangible success as quickly as possible.

External Factors

- different budgets and management structures for initiatives and innovations;

- variations in local circumstances (e.g. falling pupil rolls, scattered small towns/densely populated conurbations with inner city areas, unemployment rates);

- variations in local authority practice and precedent (some LEAs tackle every new initiative in the same way).

Box 3 seeks to relate the problems and characteristics identified in **Boxes 1** and **2** to the main **contributory factors**. One of the reasons why we opted for the term 'contributory factors' rather than 'causes' is because it is often difficult when looking at the learning problems of an individual child, as manifested at a particular point in time, to decide to what extent certain characteristics are causes of the problem or symptoms or even consequences. Take 'absence from school' as an example: prolonged absence when younger may have had an adverse effect on the child's learning of basic skills and processes. Later experiences at school reinforce the child's sense of failure which leads in turn to truancy, disruptive behaviour and the often-expressed view that school is 'boring and irrelevant'. This frustration is then perceived by the school as 'the problem' and responded to accordingly, for example, by reducing the demands made on the pupil, through 'sheltering' her or him from work which might reinforce that sense of failure, or through offering her or him an alternative, non-academic curriculum with a heavy emphasis on preparation for adult life.

In other words, what constitutes a cause, a symptom or a problem may depend upon when the school chooses to intervene in the learning cycle. Long-term persistent learning problems, if not adequately responded to before the age of 14, are more likely post-14 to be contained than resolved or remediated.

B ox 3

C O N T R I - B U T O R Y F A C T O R S

	Long-term low attainment	Short-term learning problems	Subject- or skill-specific learning difficulties	Consistent underachievement	Reluctance to learn
cumulative experience of failure in primary and early secondary years	✓				
low expectations by teachers	✓				✓
not being sufficiently 'stretched' in lessons			✓	✓	
inadequate diagnosis of learning needs at appropriate time	✓	✓	✓	✓	
inadequate monitoring and record keeping	✓	✓	✓	✓	
unrealistic demands on learners	✓			✓	
too many teachers, too many subjects, too little time	✓			✓	✓
insufficient reinforcement of learning	✓	✓	✓		✓
insufficient opportunities for individuals to discuss their work with teachers	✓	✓	✓		
timetable and course structures too inflexible to permit learners to work at own pace and thus finish assignments	✓	✓			✓
lack of short-term learning targets to reinforce learning	✓	✓		✓	✓
learning and motivational blocks about particular subjects, aspects of subjects or specific skills and processes		✓	✓		
course content and teaching methods which are insufficiently stimulating or relevant to pupils' needs	✓			✓	✓
unhelpful teaching styles and unsympathetic teaching	✓	✓		✓	
school and classroom climate further disadvantaging the least successful	✓				
insufficient attention given by some teachers to individual learning difficulties	✓	✓			✓
lack of external motivation and incentive to learn (e.g. through broader accreditation schemes, job, further education and training prospects etc.)				✓	✓
lack of parental support and encouragement	✓	✓	✓	✓	✓
unduly high expectations by parents and excessive parental pressure				✓	✓
problems at home	✓	✓		✓	
peer group pressure to conform to a norm of non-achievement	✓	✓		✓	✓
fear of success (especially among some adolescent girls)				✓	✓
changes of teacher or school		✓	✓		
sporadic attendance		✓		✓	✓
lengthy absence due to illness		✓			
social disadvantage and deprivation	✓	✓			✓

Of course there is some element of caricature in a diagram such as this. Nevertheless, it serves to highlight what are often unquestioned assumptions rather than planned strategies, and what we are seeking to do here is to encourage school planners to scrutinise and analyse their own taken-for-granted assumptions about 'the problem of lower attainment' and determine what evidence they would need to substantiate them **before** deciding on the kinds of solutions and strategies to adopt.

Box 4 relates the problems, symptoms and contributory factors to the range of **solutions** we have identified. In this context we have distinguished solutions from the mechanisms deployed to put them into practice - these form the substance of Section 3 ADDRESSING THE DIVERSITY, since how you deliver solutions is, of course, a matter for complex decision-making in itself.

Box 4

POSSIBLE SOLUTIONS

	Long-term low attainment	Short-term learning problems	Subject- or skill-specific learning difficulties	Consistent underachievement	Reluctance to learn
SEN support in classroom and, where appropriate, withdrawal	✓	✓	✓		
extra support in classroom from subject specialists	✓	✓	✓		
improved procedures for diagnosing learning needs and difficulties and for monitoring and reviewing progress	✓	✓	✓	✓	
reduced expectations and workload	✓				✓
raised expectations and workload	✓			✓	✓
changed criteria for defining and assessing attainment	✓			✓	✓
self-assessment procedures to help pupils monitor their own progress and detect their own learning problems	✓	✓	✓		
more opportunities for individually-paced and negotiated learning	✓	✓	✓		
more opportunities for counselling and guidance	✓	✓	✓		
secure and stable learning environment (e.g. base tutor system, mini-schools)	✓				
modular courses intended to provide short-term learning goals and realistic targets	✓	✓		✓	✓
reduced curriculum clutter through integrated courses and cross-curricular approaches	✓			✓	✓
supplement the curriculum with courses and cross-curricular initiatives to develop thinking skills and problem-solving skills	✓		✓	✓	
more practical, experiential and activity-based approaches to teaching and learning			✓	✓	✓
make curriculum content more relevant to post-school life				✓	✓
increase opportunities for off-site learning and working with adults other than teachers		✓		✓	✓
promote parental support for what is provided	✓			✓	✓

SECTION 2

ADDRESSING THE DIVERSITY: PROVIDING FOR LOWER ATTAINERS OR DEALING WITH LOW ATTAINMENT?

This section looks first at the range of **provision** designed to deal with low attainment, then at why schools opt for particular courses of action and at how they set about **implementing** these choices. We discuss the **pros** and **cons** of the different kinds of provision, and then give illustrations of how schools have set about implementing **responses** to the **problems** of low attainment they have identified among their own pupils.

THE PROVISION

At this point, we need to refer to **Diagram 3** (see page 32), which indicates a spectrum along which provision tends to fall. Broadly speaking, the more **targeted** the provision is, the more likely it is to depend on the prior identification and selection of 'low attaining' pupils. A targeted approach looks like a project - it is fairly easily identifiable, because it has definable boundaries. A **dispersed** approach, by contrast, is not so readily identifiable. It is usually more concerned with school organisation and management and as such tends to have implications for all pupils in the year group. Each kind of provision has its particular strengths and weaknesses, as you can see from the summary boxes.

Initiatives which tend to be deployed in a **targeted** way are:

● **alternative curriculum provision** (usually for a selected group)
This approach can be found in a large number of schools. It usually, but not always, depends on the identification of a small number of fourth and fifth year pupils for whom special provision is made. Pupils and a restricted number of teachers (usually with a commitment to and experience of this kind of work) spend a substantial part of their week together in order to meet what schools think are the primary needs of the pupils: a more relevant curriculum - often delivered through a variety of agencies (FE college, work and community experience) and based on principles of active and practical learning - and a secure environment to provide stable relationships and a fresh start for learning. Schools vary as to where they most want to innovate: by changing the curriculum (e.g. introducing integrated courses together with opportunities for off-site learning) or the environment (e.g. creating a base tutor system). Such innovations are often accompanied by alternative accreditation (see below).

impact on pupils is usually favourable, at least in terms of increased motivation and self-confidence. The flexibility of a separate timetable allows responsiveness to the group's needs. There is a strong sense of ownership for both pupils and teachers. Better relationships can develop between pupils and between pupils and teachers.

depends on pre-selecting pupils, which gives rise to the following concerns: Is all special help for fourth and fifth year pupils concentrated in this one area? If it is, it may not allow for 'coming and going' - what about pupils going through a temporary bad patch or needing subject-specific help or wanting to opt in or drop out of GCSE? Is its existence in effect a disincentive for the school to make better earlier provision of a different kind? Is it over-dependent on 'charismatic' teachers who appear to be irreplaceable? Does its emphasis on 14-16 year olds mean that it is a holding device rather than a 'solution'? Does it sometimes involve labelling pupils in a negative way?

Diagram 3

FOCUS

TARGETED	DISPERSED
Focuses on a distinct aspect of provision - pupils, teachers, subjects, skills.	**Attempts to encompass the needs of lower attainers within provision/policy for all pupils in year group/subject area/whole school.**
Often deployed in some kind of combination e.g. *alternative curriculum* for a *selected group of pupils*.	Changes may be:-*organisational* (e.g. staffing arrangements), *curricular* (e.g. involving some reconstruction of the curriculum) or *pedagogic* (e.g. involving a change in teaching styles). Different kinds of change clearly require different resourcing levels and different planning priorities; often interdependent in practice.
Targeted provision has boundaries of scale, time, staff, organisation and/or impact.	
The long-term challenge is to spread the initiative beyond its boundaries without losing the strengths and innovations acquired because of them; while avoiding the marginalisation. which is a risk with a more targeted approach.	**The long term challenge** is to ensure that changes have tangible benifits for pupils and are not confined to addressing what are in effect policy or management issues.

- **alternative courses and assessment schemes** (often for a selected group)
  These provide syllabuses or guidelines and qualifications which are thought to be more suitable for lower ability pupils by reason of their content, delivery (e.g. stress on practical learning or on short-term goals) and/or a system of accreditation (e.g. profiling). These courses may be offered to individual pupils in a subject-based curriculum as alternatives to GCSE courses, often with the possibility of dual entry. Alternatively, they may be offered as a way of structuring and accrediting a version of the alternative curriculum (see above).

allows pupils either to acquire new knowledge and skills and thus refresh their attitude to education or to tackle traditional subjects in a more flexible way. Gives credit for what has been achieved (if accreditation is criterion-referenced) as opposed to reaffirming a sense of failure. Either supports and reinforces an alternative curriculum or, in the case of 'dual entry' approach, creates a safety net with minimal disruption to the timetable. Gives credibility to pupils' work outside their school.

may create, or rather perpetuate, a 'second class' system of qualification (e.g. 'profiles are for thick kids' or 'bright kids don't get pre-voc qualifications'). Raises issues of marketing to pupils, to parents and to end-users ('is this a worthwhile or a Mickey Mouse qualification?'). Whilst overcoming some of the problems of a traditional 'mainstream' curriculum (by being, for example, more practical or experiential), subject-based courses may reproduce other problems of the traditional ' mainstream' curriculum, such as fragmentation and lack of coherence.

- **structured learning strategies,** such as Thinking Skills (sometimes for a selected group)
  Approaches such as Thinking Skills have been designed in order to help pupils become aware of, and so improve, the way they learn. There is accordingly an emphasis on problem-solving and decision-making. In some cases the strategy is adopted by a group of subject teachers in their own lessons, though it is also taught as a separate slot in the curriculum, on the principle that once they become aware of what they're doing, pupils will be able readily to transfer these skills to other situations.

this approach may re-motivate pupils through the use of novel and challenging activities. If pursued in conjunction with a problem-solving approach across the curriculum, it can give fresh point to what pupils are doing and help them to take more control of their own learning. It can encourage them to be more aware of how they learn, and their own strengths and weaknesses.

it may end up being seen by teachers and pupils as a gimmick, especially if it is taught as an isolated 'subject'. The process of transfer of skills from one activity or curriculum area to another is not yet precisely understood, so the extent of impact of this kind of initiative may be more limited than its proponents claim. Some monitoring of transfer to other lessons seems to be essential, but there is not much evidence of this happening.

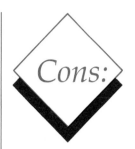

- **in-class support for individual pupils**
  Alongside the integration of special needs provision in the classroom, many schools are providing additional support for identified pupils by timetabling subject teachers, on a voluntary or allocated basis, to act in a support role, whether in their own or other subject lessons. Special needs and support provision is usually organised in the lower school, but clearly this has implications for supporting GCSE work too.

individual pupils can receive the help they need without being withdrawn and labelled; they can also get subject-specific help from a specialist. It allows support staff to work with groups as well as individuals or to teach the class while the other teacher takes a small group - in other words it permits flexibility. It also encourages all staff to take responsibility for pupils' learning needs and difficulties. It enables inter-departmental identification of problems and monitoring of progress. Even where this does not lead to team-teaching as such, it can break down the barriers of 'the closed classroom' i.e. one classroom/one teacher.

it may reinforce negative labelling if the support teacher is too obviously identified with particular pupil(s). The choice and in-service training of those adopting a support role needs careful thought and organisation. If done on an allocated basis (depending on free slots in the timetable) support teachers may be reluctant to put in the effort required to monitor and address pupils' needs, especially if they are supporting a subject with which they are unfamiliar. Teachers may find colleagues' presence threatening and find ways of opting out. Unless time is found outside lessons for planning, the in-class support may be *ad hoc* and not particularly effective.

Examples of initiatives which tend to be more **dispersed** are:

- **reconstruction of the curriculum**
  Some schools have taken the step of reconstructing the curriculum for a whole year group. Three distinct strategies emerge:

- the *integrated curriculum,* which takes different forms according to whether the curriculum is planned around cross-curricular themes or skills or concepts or even, most recently, attainment targets (a move which some schools are now actively considering, at least for the non-core areas of the curriculum);

- the *modular curriculum,* where the curriculum, or significant areas of it, is broken down into short-term self-contained modules within or across traditional subject boundaries;

- the *entitlement curriculum,* interpreted in a variety of ways, but broadly aiming to offer the same coherent and balanced curriculum and learning experiences to all pupils.

the *integrated curriculum* offers exciting possibilities for breaking down artificial subject barriers and working on common themes, skills, etc. and for motivating pupils and helping them take charge of their own learning by offering a package which makes more sense to them. Integrated curricula are often used to facilitate the transition from primary to secondary sectors. A *modular curriculum* offers short-term and hence achievable learning goals, variety and intensity. Like the integrated curriculum, it can permit pupils to work at their own pace. The *entitlement curriculum* offers equality of access and protects some pupils from getting a 'second class deal' by being offered a different kind of curriculum, with different outcomes, from the rest. It also offers a less cluttered timetable with fewer options and greater emphasis on core and basic skills.

the *integrated curriculum* can become a management exercise whose objectives are clear in the minds of managers, less clear to some of the teachers and not at all clear to the pupils, partly because they could make sense of the new curriculum only in terms of what had gone before. Much depends, therefore, on what kind of curriculum pupils are familiar with. A *modular curriculum* may have little clear progression and coherence in it, but remains a series of disparate subjects or discrete units tacked together end on. There may be insufficient time to do justice to a topic, so pupils' interest is never fully engaged. Specialist teachers may not feel that they can teach to the same standard all aspects of, for instance, an integrated science course. Relationships with pupils may not have time to take root, giving rise to problems of motivation. The *entitlement curriculum* may exist in name only; it needs other systems and structures to be in place, such as provision for support teaching, adequate staffing and/or procedures for monitoring pupils' progress closely. To be effective, however, it also needs a major re-think of prevailing teaching styles.

- **reorganisation of staff roles and responsibilities**
  This approach is designed to encourage all staff to become involved in the review and reform of the curriculum, pedagogy and/or pastoral responsibilities. In particular it may be used to identify and make use of good innovators on the staff who may not be highly placed within the hierarchy.

this approach can be exciting and stimulating for teachers if they are intensively involved in professional development on a number of fronts; it may change the way people see their subject and/or their role. It can make effective (i.e. progressive, coherent, self-directed) use of INSET programmes. It can lead to new kinds of staff development.

the approach needs to be handled sensitively and with due regard for pressures on teachers' time and their vulnerabilities in a climate of stress and low morale (due to the pace of change, falling rolls, bad press coverage, 'innovation fatigue' etc.). It must be premised on generally good relationships between staff and management. It may not have tangible effect on pupils and their performance for some time (and it is difficult to ascribe any such changes to this particular cause).

● **reorganisation of school information systems and procedures**
Schools may want, for example, to improve their provision for monitoring and assessing every pupil, which entails refining the recording, transferring and retrieving procedures for this information. It also means staff need to realise the importance of the information for addressing pupils' different and changing learning needs - much of this information at present is theoretically accessible, but often languishes in filing cabinets in different departments or in the head of year's office, or is accessible to pastoral but not academic staff, or vice versa. Some schools are operating with insufficient information; it needs expanding and refining. Communication and liaison networks with parents and the wider community, for example, may also come under scrutiny.

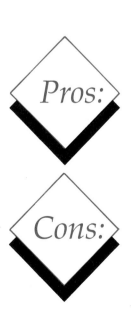

this exercise may reveal surprising and significant facts about individual pupils, such as that their actual performance in particular subjects is high, though their attendance is poor. It may also alert staff to recurrent problems first identified at primary stage. Profiling is clearly giving a boost to this kind of change.

this approach may degenerate into tinkering with a system for no clear reason. Different departments may continue to operate independent and mutually incompatible systems. Information collected must be put to use and this is more likely to happen if other aspects of the school are coming under review, such as provision of support teaching or staff responsibilities (see above).

Some initiatives can be **targeted** or **dispersed** depending on the school's curricular and organisational priorities, such as:

- **changing the social and physical environment for learning**
  Many secondary schools have taken a leaf from the primary book by putting up displays of pupils' work (and not just 'the best') and re-arranging classrooms, for instance to enable group work rather than lessons dominated by teachers talking. These changes are often most noticeable in project group areas, but need not, of course, be confined to them. Some schools have taken steps to make the general environment less formal, for example by installing a coffee bar or by changing school opening times to encourage early morning and late afternoon social use of the premises.

these measures may enhance overall commitment and motivation on the part of both pupils and staff, and help to break down barriers between somewhat artificial routines of institutional life and informal peer group culture.

these are background rather than foreground changes; they do nothing to address individual pupils' learning needs. Changes to classroom environment need to be made in the context of considered teaching and learning strategies rather than as something of unquestionable value in their own right.

- **new pedagogy via selected teachers**
  Some projects have identified particular aspects of the curriculum which have been traditionally underplayed in schools - one example is *oracy*, that is, the encouragement of talk in the classroom not only from teacher to pupil but from pupils to teacher and between pupils in group work. Oracy therefore has a number of separate aspects:

  - ❏ encouraging pupils to internalise their grasp of concepts, issues, problems, etc. through the act of turning them into their own words either individually or in groups;

  - ❏ promoting active and participatory learning;

  - ❏ encouraging non-directive teaching methods;

  - ❏ promoting cross-curricular change and inter-departmental collaboration;

  - ❏ using oral expression as part of the assessment of achievement.

But above all, this approach, like that of active learning, argues that in order for pupils to change, teachers must change first. Most initiatives contain some element of staff development, of course, but in this type of provision staff development is a primary objective.

this work may be highly intensive for teachers and heighten their job satisfaction; it gives them a context within which to review their own work and that of close colleagues. It also introduces new ways of working to the pupils, which can increase their self-confidence and motivation. There is a strong sense of ownership among staff and a sense of controlling their own learning for the pupils. Feedback from oracy work makes teachers more pupil-centred; they realise how much pupils already know and where their real problems lie.

unless clear objectives are set, the initiative may develop in an unco-ordinated fashion - lots of ideas, but no defined goals or structure - which detracts from its overall effectiveness. The cascade model of spreading innovations tends to be ineffective unless the key teachers are in a position to stimulate change within the institution. They may end up as specialist teachers within the school, when the original aim was eventually to equip all teachers with cross-curricular awareness and skills. As with the reconstructed curriculum, pupils may have difficulty adjusting to new expectations on them: is it 'real work'? There may be additional pressure on teachers as the ethos for class discipline changes.

You can see that there is a potential tension (which may, of course, be fruitful) between a targeted strategy and mainstream provision. A careful course must be steered between being over-protective of what has been established and diluting the initiative's potential for effecting real and lasting change by integrating it prematurely into the mainstream. You can see what this means in practice by looking at the case studies in Section 4, particularly Broomhill and Green Lane.

By contrast, initiatives taking a dispersed route to implementation and thereby, for instance, encompassing all the pupils in a year group, sometimes seem to have little impact on pupils' actual learning needs and problems. This is because they are often more concerned with offering solutions to management issues. However, this kind of systemic change has, as we shall see, a role to play in the formulation of whole school strategies.

THE SCHOOLS: IMPLEMENTING THE PROVISION

The schools appearing here figured in the earlier portraits of schools on pages 17-20 and you may like to refer back to those, recalling that the first four, **Bankside**, **Broomhill**, **Green Lane** and **Fairacre**, are discussed in greater depth than the rest. Additionally, the later sections, on management issues (MAKING IT WORK, starting on page 47) and on whole school strategies (TOWARDS A WHOLE SCHOOL STRATEGY FOR RAISING ATTAINMENT, starting on page 67) pick up the same stories at subsequent stages in their development.

The following narratives are designed to suggest, with the benefit of hindsight (things are rarely that clear at the time), why schools opted for particular initiatives, how they went about implementing them and whether the type of provision they chose was an appropriate **response** to the kinds of **problem** relating to low attainment they had and the general solutions they were proposing. In most cases, while adhering broadly to the approach promoted by the LEA, schools took the opportunity to opt for what appeared to be the most appropriate means of addressing their own specific situations.

As we remarked in the first section, as far as many individual case study schools were concerned, the identification of problems, solutions and appropriate provision was all rather piecemeal. (It is possible that the uncertainty over funding may have been a contributory factor. As the complementary policy report *Investing in Reform* observes, the phasing of grants did not happen in the most effective way to encourage planned development either at LEA or school level.)

In **Bankside School** the **problem** revolved around the high proportion (75 per cent) of pupils with low scores on cognitive ability tests, the relatively large number of statemented pupils and a catchment area of long-standing social deprivation. The **response** was to use LAPP funding to undertake a restructuring of the third (i.e. intake) year curriculum, to make it more integrated and practical.

Over the three years of the initiative, each successive year saw a development or a re-working of the 'integration' approach as various issues emerged. In the first year, the team consisted of eight staff and a co-ordinator, each of whom was made available for up to six double periods a week to work with any third form teacher. This entailed giving additional classroom support and developing and teaching integrated or cross-curricular units. In the following year, provision for integration was more structured, being limited to two of the third form groups, who were offered an integrated curriculum. The timetable was rearranged so that each course would be taught by three staff, each from a different department, who were expected to develop integrated units. For 1988-89, the Senior Management Team (SMT) decided that, with the exception of a 'fast stream' of the fifteen most able pupils, the rest of the year group should be timetabled for the integrated

SECTION 3

curriculum with teams of three staff, representing three different subject areas, teaching the equivalent of two tutor groups. Each version of integration encouraged some form of collaboration among departments, for example, and more experiential forms of teaching/ learning.

But at the end of three years there was no consensus amongst teachers of either the value or the definition of an 'integrated curriculum' nor was there a coherent policy concerning the changing roles of teachers expected to work in cross-curricular teams. You can see from this how the characteristic advantages and disadvantages of the **integrated curriculum** *outlined on page 35 above apply to the situation in Bankside.*

When in 1983 **Broomhill High School** was nominated by its LEA to participate in LAPP, it adopted a strategy broadly in line with the one being promoted by the LEA's central team. The **problem** was seen as some pupils' failure to achieve in school, whether through absence, lack of confidence or ability, or because they had become disaffected. The **response** was based on promoting an alternative curriculum programme more tailored to the learning needs of those pupils.

The key elements in the LEA's approach were:

❑ *the development of modular courses*

❑ *accumulated credit schemes and records of achievement*

❑ *learning by doing and practical problem-solving*

❑ *development of work-related skills*

❑ *residentials, work experience, community placements and FE link courses.*

Emphasis was also given to the need for building good relationships between project staff and pupils, and to developing the scope for project pupils to negotiate their own individual curricula supported by ' contracts' between learners and their teachers. Broomhill, along with a few other project schools in the LEA, decided that the best means for delivering this kind of alternative curriculum would be through what they described as 'a base tutor system'. The approach - borrowed from primary education - involved putting lower attaining pupils into small classes with a form tutor who would work with them for approximately half the week. The rest of the week was spent in option groups with the rest of the year or on skills courses with specialist teachers and volunteers in order to pursue interests such as typing, computing, budgeting, electronic music-making.

The base tutors' role was to teach English, mathematics and PSE, accompany pupils on residentials, organise group and individual projects, act as counsellors and generally take on the responsibilities of a form teacher. In the first year approximately 80 fourth and 80 fifth formers were selected for the alternative curriculum - about one-third of the year group. Pupils were nominated by staff. Most of those selected had five or more nominations, but were free to opt out if they and their parents chose. The project staff consisted of a co-ordinator and eight base tutors. Although the PTR was therefore 20:1 groups were usually much smaller than this due to selective absenteeism. Additional money (from LAPP) was used primarily for 2.5 extra staff, some new equipment and the running costs of residentials, FE link courses and other out-of-school activities and the annual costs incurred by alternative accreditation schemes.

Some major changes occurred over the lifetime of the initiative. Perhaps the most significant was that in 1986 when the head and SMT, partly in response to GCSE but also in response to open enrolment provision in the 1986 Education Act, decided that all project pupils should do some GCSE courses. Mathematics was to be taught in sets by specialist teachers (so project pupils tended to remain in the same group but with an unfamiliar teacher); integrated science was to be taught in mixed ability groups by specialists; whilst English GCSE was to be taught by the base tutors, only one of whom was an English teacher. These changes are instructive in showing how **alternative curriculum provision** *may have unforeseen vulnerabilities, particularly during a period of major externally imposed change. How do you preserve its advantages, while making it more flexible?*

Green Lane School adopted a **response** not unlike that of Broomhill, that is to say an alternative curriculum for a small proportion (10-15 per cent) of fourth and fifth years selected for the project on account of persistent difficulties in school. The initial **problem** was rather different, though. The organisation and curriculum of the school was at that time fairly traditional. At the beginning, pupils were selected for the project as much because they were truanting or disruptive in class as because they had learning difficulties.

The project became a last resort for pupils who didn't or wouldn't fit in with the academically-oriented curriculum. The project leader in the school had previously worked with RoSLA pupils, and developed an expertise both in organising a 'relevant' curriculum for older pupils and in relating well to groups and individuals whose previous experiences of school had been pretty negative. He made a practice of visiting pupils at home with their parents and involving parents in the project wherever possible. The LEA, meanwhile, gave active backing to the project and the central team, consisting of only two staff and an administrator/secretary, adopted a personal, committed and 'up-front' approach to giving support and guidance. This was probably crucial to the continuation of the project in Green Lane - a crisis point was reached after a couple of years, basically because the project had manifestly become a sin-bin. Much of the project leader's time was spent 'chasing kids, trying to get them to come to school' and in policing them once they were there. For a few pupils, the curriculum was being shaped not by their needs, but by the necessity to control their behaviour during off-site activities (college link courses, work placements). Parents and tutors of low-achieving, but quiet children occasionally wondered about the benefit of having them selected for the project. Loud-mouthed lads predominated, and the project teachers had to get used to non-project colleagues bending their ear about the latest enormity 'their' pupils had perpetrated. Staff morale on the project fell at one point, perhaps especially since such good things had been predicted for the project at county level after a great deal of favourable publicity. On the suggestion of the county team leader the identification and selection criteria for project pupils were clarified and tightened. Instead of the general criterion of failure to thrive in the system, a combination of NFER Tests AH2 and AH3, middle school records, reports from support teachers, form and subject tutors and attendance and attitude data were compiled into a database of indices of need. This change resulted in the project intake matching the school's intake, in socio-economic terms, more closely: social and behavioural problems did not dominate project activities. The project settled down into an apparently sustainable pattern: clear selection criteria, a curriculum based on the acquisition of practical, social and basic academic skills delivered through a multi-agency approach and accredited through a CGLI-endorsed profile. The project, originally housed in a mobile classroom 'at the other end of the playing field', was moved to a newly-furnished suite of rooms in a wing of the school building; relationships between project staff and pupils became better and more trusting; good relations were built with the local community and employers and project staff no longer regarded their appointment as a dead-end. The project advisory group, consisting of project staff, a school governor, a councillor, parents and representatives of the local community, continued to meet regularly for mutual information and support. The job placement record was good; former pupils came back to visit; the project had established itself as a feasible and successful innovation, at least in its own terms.

*Nonetheless, there remained some unresolved endemic issues - like, where did the disruptives go? What if project pupils wanted to take GCSE courses? Who had ownership of, and/or responsibility for, the project? - which turned into acute problems as a combination of falling rolls and the impending requirements of LMS impelled the school management to reconsider, first, their priorities for staffing and second, the reorganisation of the academic/pastoral structures into faculties. Such questions further illustrate the sort of factors school planners need to bear in mind if **alternative curriculum provision** is being considered as an option, especially for 14-16 year olds.*

It could be said that at one time **Fairacre School** had been an underachieving, school: it had an endemic **problem** of motivation among its lower ability pupils, who formed quite a large proportion of the intake. The county's initiative, an alternative assessment and accreditation scheme aimed at pupils for whom a diet consisting only of GCSEs was deemed unsuitable, had been adopted, subject by subject, as a **response** in the major curriculum areas in this school.

Modern languages and humanities (for which the GCSE course in Integrated Humanities was assessed entirely on course work) were at this time not included. The school project co-ordinator, who was also one of the two deputy heads, was firmly committed to the principles of the scheme, in so far as it enabled pupils of low academic ability to follow mainstream courses and to gain a recognised qualification for doing so. So that when the school's intake began to reflect the whole ability spectrum, on account of its increasing popularity with parents, a range of these alternative courses continued to be offered. Each year there tended to be a small number of pupils taking alternative courses in three, four or more subjects, including mathematics, science and English; but nearly half the year group would take at least one course. Departments differed in their organisation of these courses as well as in their associated teaching strategies, though on the whole they managed to involve most staff in teaching them. In mathematics and English, the alternative course was taught to the bottom set or sets (which were kept small), whereas the science department taught the alternative course alongside the GCSE course in larger mixed ability groups. These differences had implications for the selection of pupils for courses - broadly speaking, the less segregated the groups, the more chance there was for flexibility. Decisions about whether a pupil taking science (which was an integrated course) should be entered for GCSE or the alternative qualification could be delayed until the fifth year, for example. By contrast, 'alternative courses' in local studies (taught by the geography department) and outdoor pursuits (PE) were offered across the ability range as part of the options scheme. Pupils' achievements were recorded by means of a detailed subject profile, for which systematic moderating and certificating procedures had been set up by the county team. The certificates awarded to pupils in consequence of successfully completing a course were endorsed by one of the examining boards and had won a degree of recognition in the eyes of local employers.

As has been indicated above, there are conspicuous advantages in this kind of initiative: pupils got the chance to make progress and gain certification in a subject where their chances of getting a good GCSE grade were slim, whilst not being segregated into an identifiable group; arguably it also increased the job satisfaction of subject specialist teachers, who were freed from the constraints of an examination syllabus inappropriate to the needs of low ability pupils, while at the same time the initiative as a whole was minimally disruptive to the organisation of the school's departmental timetables.

*What this meant in practice, however, was that the day-to-day operation of **alternative course provision** mirrored the strengths and weaknesses of its institutional environment. Particular issues which arose concerned the relationship of lower and upper school curricula and support provision; the interpretation and administration of profiling; the degree of collaboration among departments over appropriate teaching strategies for lower ability pupils.*

Other schools perceived the **problem** in different ways: in **Robinswood High School** it was identified as a multi-faceted one, where getting on for two-fifths of pupils scored low on cognitive ability tests, and many had severe behavioural difficulties too. An appropriate **response** would not lie in attempting to offer distinct provision to low attainers, but in boosting their skills and learning strategies through a common entitlement curriculum enhanced by a range of cross-curricular activities and experiences.

The head described the underlying principle as follows: 'Traditional subject areas are still accepted as the main contributions to learning. They can promote a rich variety of knowledge, concepts and skills. They form the "warp" of the curriculum. Common to all these traditional areas are other vital experiences, such as active learning methods, which cross boundaries and assist in integrating the curriculum. This is the "weft". Together the "warp" and the "weft" form a coherent curriculum.' In this school, the 'weft' has taken the form of six cross-curricular elements: residentials, social and life skills, communication skills, using the community as a resource for learning, post-school experience and assessment and profiling. The intake year is organised on a mixed ability basis; at the end of the year each faculty groups pupils according to its own policy. This has led to some fairly unusual developments. For example, mathematics and science do not set whilst humanities does. In the fourth and fifth years the pupils are expected to take GCSEs in English, mathematics, recreational studies and PSE. 'Optional' GCSEs have to include at least one science, one humanities subject and a creative art in addition to three other choices. When the school first embarked on LAPP the lowest attainers (about 35 pupils) were permanently grouped in remedial sets, but in 1988 the head of special needs discontinued this practice and replaced it with in-class support.

A major and persistent **problem** of low attainment and underachievement among a large number of the 350 pupils in **City Road Comprehensive** had no doubt stemmed from the wider socio-economic problems of the area and were exacerbated by the constant threat of school closure. It was felt nothing less than a whole school approach would offer an appropriate **response.**

This took the form of reorganising the curriculum into an entitlement curriculum, based on practical and skills-based learning and delivered through modular courses, and systematic development of teachers' understanding and skills. A group of teachers was given secondment to take a part-time MA in curriculum development at the local polytechnic and to review their own professional practices. The insights gained were intended to be fed back into the curriculum development process in the school.

In another school, the **problem** was seen as a dual one - what to offer, by way of attainable goals, to a small proportion of fourth and fifth year pupils who would be taking a limited number of GCSEs; and how better to identify and address the learning needs of pupils all the way through their secondary school career. The **response** was seen by the head and a number of key staff in **The King's School** in terms of a whole school approach.

Though it was not one of the LEA's pilot schools, the school had become involved with LAPP as the county initiative changed its policy from a cohort-based approach to a whole school approach based on differentiation. The school too had moved from a traditional remedial model of provision for lower attainers to a more integrated approach: a foundation course to be offered as an option to fourth and fifth years alongside their core studies, and a better overall co-ordination of pupil support, both academic and pastoral, directed by the philosophy that all pupils should have equal access to all aspects of the curriculum.

This was supported by the initiation of a profiling scheme for recording pupils' achievement; departments were working independently with a view to co-ordinating their respective developments, though it was not clear how this would happen. During the academic year, the county team of advisory teachers had supported both the establishment of the foundation course and the development of profiling particularly within the science department. Additionally, the county was in the process of redefining the roles and responsibilities of special needs staff; the new post of pupil support co-ordinator (replacing a 'remedial department' approach to special needs) was an innovation in this direction. The person appointed was committed to a whole school approach to an entitlement curriculum and took a pro-active line in developing links with colleagues.

The approach of **Little Stoke School** was rather different from the others: in one sense it had not identified a **problem** of low attainment as such. But it had taken the opportunity, offered by the LEA's initiative, to develop oracy work, ostensibly because it was felt pupils were leaving school with somewhat inadequate skills in this area - they weren't doing themselves justice with potential employers. It appeared that the project, as a **response,** was geared more towards institutional than to pupil change.

The methodology of teaching came under scrutiny, underscored by the kinds of change TVEI was making towards active learning and negotiation. Accordingly, pupils were not selected for the project; they became involved according to which subject teachers were participating in the project and which classes they thought oracy might usefully contribute to. Two school co-ordinators, one a scientist and HoD, the other an English teacher, were funded for half a day a week each to develop oracy with their own classes and to look for ways of spreading the developments to other staff and other departments. This 'two-pronged' approach was a potentially powerful one, because it involved different departments simultaneously and staff at different levels in the hierarchy. Other staff from most departments became involved in initiating oracy work with some of their classes and in the process reviewing their own teaching goals and strategies. But some of these staff came to the project with more experience than others, and the individual, voluntary nature of staff participation meant that it was initially difficult for developments to be systematically spread either within departments or even to other classes taught by teachers participating in the oracy initiative.

> The descriptions of schools you have been reading should be useful in showing how the implementation of provision is, on the one hand, related closely to how the school perceives the problem initially, but how, on the other, it may impel schools to modify their conception of what that problem really is.

So far the descriptions have provided what amounts to a series of snapshots of what is, after all, a *process.* In the next section, MAKING IT WORK, we take the stories forward, so you can see what happens to the strategy for differentiation as it becomes established, and also what contribution (positive or negative) it makes to the school's overall policy for change.

MAKING

IT WORK: CHANGE IN THE SCHOOL OR CHANGING THE SCHOOL?

In this section we are looking in some detail at questions of **school management,** those tactical and strategic considerations which follow on from initiating and implementing provision for dealing with low attainment: how is the initiative to be consolidated and built on, given that schools are hierarchical institutions to a greater or lesser degree, with structures which may or may not be conducive at the time to the kinds of change intended?

Some further illustrations from our four main case study schools, **Bankside**, **Broomhill**, **Green Lane**, and **Fairacre**, will clarify what we think may be entailed in the interactive process between initiative and institution. These narrative extracts are intended to illustrate different ways in which change can be generated or impeded, its momentum sustained or slowed, and conditions created or missed for spreading good practice. Each extract is followed by a **review** which draws together the salient points from the longer-term development of the initiative in that school.

The kinds of management issues identified in these and other schools appear in the form of **questions** which will be useful to school planners and managers considering the longer-term implications and impact of initiatives concerned with tackling the problems of differentiation and attainment.

A useful starting point for any such discussion is those constraints and problems which school managers typically encounter. In Section 1, we observed that schools are subject to a number of external and internal pressures which act as a brake on innovation. We can summarise the major internal constraints as follows:

- **ingrained assumptions and practices**
Ingrained assumptions and practices have the power to override educational intentions. For example, despite widespread discussion and apparent acceptance of ideas such as criterion referencing, self-assessment and a broader concept of achievement, there is still a widespread and persistent inclination for teachers - and other educationalists - to employ a one-dimensional view of ability based on the 'norm' when talking about 'lower attainers'. This is not surprising, since virtually everyone does at some time or another. In other words, an underlying norm-referenced concept of general ability may in practice be used as the key factor in making organisational decisions, such as setting or grouping pupils, or in informally sizing up a 'mixed ability' class. Ingrained assumptions of this kind can also affect classroom practices. So - for example - approaches designed to maximise the individual's responsibility for her own learning sometimes founder on the reluctance of teachers to relinquish control of the learning process or to change their over-dominant teaching style.

- **pragmatic adjustments to the school's organisational priorities**

Organisational constraints can exert undue power in tempting schools to define and tie down problems within manageable boundaries where they can be dealt with, preferably without upsetting the rest of the institutional framework. In some schools, there are always strong pressures to make the innovation conform to the requirements of existing structures and organisational procedures (such as timetables or the departmental/pastoral framework) even when to do so is to limit the potential impact of the innovation.

- **limited procedures for identifying learning needs and problems**

Schools vary somewhat in this respect. At one end of the spectrum are those which make a decision about the ability level of each pupil in the intake year based on information supplied by the feeder schools (including their reading ages) and then band them accordingly for their secondary education. At the other end are those schools (far fewer in number) which systematically and regularly monitor the progress across the curriculum of each child and diagnose her or his individual learning needs and problems, not just in the first year but throughout each child's school career.

- **project framework**

Strictly speaking, this is neither an internal nor an external constraint, but a hybrid, operating both from within and outside the institution. While 'project framework' is clearly a relevant factor only when there is some outside influence - whether in the shape of money, policy, or the systematic development of an initiative by an LEA or other extra-institutional team (or all three in combination) - there is a wide range of such influences which bring pressure to bear on schools' practices, both positively and negatively. Funded initiatives can produce additional problems: the project framework together with the perceived pressure to produce 'results' in a short time sometimes means simplifying the definition of the task in some way or selecting only an aspect of it to develop. The expectations and preconceptions of the project held by non-project staff sooner or later come home to roost, as it were; and success can be as detrimental to further experimentation as 'failure'. Furthermore, as we have said, initiatives of this kind have tended to be primarily aimed at older pupils (14-16) so that diagnostic procedures or teaching/learning strategies thought of as appropriate for the 11-14 age range are often not taken into account. Hence, in some cases, there is effectively a resistance to the incorporation of special needs staff into project development.

Readers may regard the issue of resourcing, as it emerges in the case studies, as being a project-specific constraint, and in one sense, clearly that is true. During the first three years of LAPP one school, for example, received £36,000 additional funding, sufficient for 2.5 extra staff, FE link courses, residentials, extra equipment and transport; whereas by 1988-89 the additional funding had been cut to just over £2,000 a year with consequent problems for the whole alternative curriculum approach in the school. However, most school-based innovations require some re-allocation of resources - if not financial, then human or material. The key question for school management is how long they would be prepared to sustain the level of resourcing which a new initiative seems to require before deciding that it has to stand on its own feet.

Note how these issues keep recurring in the continuing stories of our schools and their attempts to provide adequately for their underachieving pupils.

THE SCHOOLS: MANAGING AND DEVELOPING THE INNOVATIONS

BANKSIDE

In **Bankside School** the curriculum implementation strategy has been one of 'softly softly'. The head and SMT believe that whole school change is a long and often painful business; sometimes a process of 'one step forward and two steps back'. The results in the first year of the integrated curriculum for third years were patchy. Some departments were reluctant to get involved. Even where positive attempts to integrate were made, they tended to take the form of inter-disciplinary collaboration for a specific unit or class project rather than genuine integration. Organisational changes in the second year of the initiative turned out once again to have mixed results. Success or failure depended to a large degree on who was timetabled to work together and this was determined by the deputy head in charge of timetabling. The deputy's priorities were the staffing of GCSE and the City and Guilds course. This meant that the previous year's project team - the ones most experienced at integrated teaching - were not all available for third year teaching. Furthermore, the timetable threw up some unlikely liaisons such as home economics, maths and geography; history, French and art. The emerging picture from the third year, with its greater emphasis on team work, was once again mixed. More staff were now experienced in cross-curricular collaboration, and some had changed their teaching styles to accommodate more emphasis on practical and experiential learning. The introduction of a RoA with greater emphasis on monitoring the progress of individual pupils and the establishment of formal planning links with the school's TVEI team gave greater coherence and direction to the process of reconstructing the third year curriculum. But the role of the support teacher, i.e. the third member of the trio who 'floated' between the two tutor groups, varied considerably. Occasional collaboration was still more *common than genuine integration. Just as the school was beginning to come to terms with some of these issues, the LEA introduced its reorganisation plan, offered an enhanced premature retirement plan to staff over 50 years of age and redeployment to other staff. This meant that some of the third year teaching staff involved in the integrated curriculum left half-way through the year. Reorganisation also removed the extra staffing, increased the timetable commitments of the rest of the staff and necessitated severe cuts in the time which had previously been available for planning and development meetings, including the development of integrated units.*

Review: Bankside School has concentrated on making the kinds of organisational and procedural changes that should facilitate widespread curriculum change, and this has undoubtedly been helped by extra funding and overstaffing. But what was lacking was any coherent thinking and planning about the process of integration itself, for example:

❏   whether to integrate around content, themes, issues, concepts, skills;

❏   whether to integrate through projects, teaching materials, worksheets;

❏   how to integrate learning with assessment;

❏   how to give pupils a sense of purpose and direction in a curriculum which looks very different from the one with which they are familiar.

BROOMHILL

*In **Broomhill High School** likewise, substantial changes to the alternative curriculum approach had occurred over the first six years of its development. First of all, most of the eight base tutors who had taken the first cohort of pupils through their fourth and fifth years were not available to teach the second cohort. The project co-ordinator was faced with the task of 'breaking in' a whole new group of tutors, but without an effective induction programme. One of the head's responses to this was to appoint two primary-trained teachers and to reduce the number of tutor groups from four to three in each year. Then in 1986 the head and SMT, partly in response to GCSE but also in response to the open enrolment provision in the 1986 Education Act, decided that all project pupils should do some GCSE courses. The overall effect of this was to erode the time, by up to 50 per cent, spent by project pupils with their base tutor.*

This brought to the fore a number of problems. Tutors were teaching GCSE subjects for which they had received little or no training. The base tutor groups were being taught as groups and the pace of lessons was pitched to that of the slowest learner and yet most tutor groups contained a fairly wide ability range since some pupils had been selected for their disruptive tendencies rather than their learning problems. On the other hand, attempts to return brighter project pupils to the mainstream proved problematic because they liked the security of the base. As a solution, therefore, it proved to be neither a 'safety net' for drop-outs nor a 'trampoline' to bounce them back into the mainstream curriculum.

Beyond a certain point - half-way through - in the fourth year, it was difficult to get into GCSE courses, and just as difficult for mainstream pupils to opt out of GCSE and into the alternative curriculum. For the next cohort the number of pupils selected for the alternative curriculum has been cut, and there will be only two base tutor groups in the fourth year. This would seem to represent a shift towards the project becoming the provision for the bottom 20 per cent of the ability range - a response in part to pressure from HoDs who want to maximise their entry rates for GCSE whilst minimising their failure rates. It has also been decided that the timetable allocation for base tutor work will be restored to 50 per cent of the week. In other words, this reduced group of low ability pupils will be effectively removed from the mainstream.

But back in 1983, there were good reasons for supposing that the first eight base tutors would become a vanguard for change within the school. If you refer back to page 50 you will see that initially the teachers involved in the alternative curriculum approach laid as much emphasis on the introduction of active and experiential learning and teaching methods as on the introduction of a system of base tutors. At that stage the initiative was not conceived as being a special needs withdrawal unit operating under another name (although there were elements of this). It was assumed that the tutors would be the vanguard or pilot testers for a different approach to teaching and learning, which ultimately would be beneficial for all pupils in the school. As you can see, it has not worked out that way.

Three important factors can be identified: the tutors' own perceptions of their role, their colleagues' perceptions of the alternative curriculum and the fact that after three years of LAPP funding the extra resources were drastically reduced. The base tutors tended to see the teaching and learning approaches they employed with project pupils as tailored to those pupils' particular needs. When they taught mainstream classes, most adopted a more traditional style of teaching. This was most noticeable when comparing lessons in the base with their GCSE specialist classes. Equally, their colleagues who had not participated in the alternative curriculum initiative seldom recognised its potential for their own teaching. For most of them, it was a heaven-sent opportunity to off-load the awkward squad. Finally, the phasing out of external LAPP funding led to what the school co-ordinator described as 'an impoverished curriculum' compared with what had previously been on offer.

Review: Broomhill's approach, as a solution to the particular problem which it originally identified, has been only partially successful. It could be said that most of the pros outlined for the alternative curriculum provision on page 32 did indeed emerge. Potentially it was a highly effective way of meeting the needs of those pupils in any year group who feel insecure and lack the confidence in mainstream classes and can benefit from more stable relationships with fewer teachers. This calls for systematic diagnosis and monitoring of pupils and also for in-service training for the staff. Without these, it is not surprising if teachers involved with alternative curriculum provision see themselves as glorified childminders, lacking status within the school and probably putting their career chances at risk. Perhaps the main lesson here is that it is usually easier to institutionalise structures, systems and management or organisational innovations than it is to institutionalise ideas and new teaching styles and practices.

GREEN LANE

By 1987, **Green Lane School** had apparently developed a viable long-term form of provision for fourth and fifth year underachievers, though certain issues remained unresolved. For example, although project pupils were dispersed throughout mixed ability tutor groups, in practice some of them behaved more like a segregated group making their way to the project rooms as soon after registration as they could and spending lunch-time there if they could. This was certainly partly due to the relaxed and informal atmosphere created by project staff, but was also probably an expression of the stable and on the whole mutually trusting relationships that had developed. This separate identity was reinforced by the fact that though project pupils were taught by non-project staff in science, CDT and PE could in theory be taught in mixed ability groups, but were in practice taught in their project groups on non-GCSE courses. No doubt timetabling played a part in this, as did the notional desirability of integrating these specialist courses with the humanities, PSE and mathematics work undertaken on the project. However, specialist subject staff did not, on the whole, discuss their proposed courses with project staff in any detail. The project staff were not only responsible for running the project, they were also doing much of the pastoral work that was the nominal responsibility of form tutors or heads of year. All this further reinforced the 'boundaries' between the project and the rest of the school.

This situation was allowed to develop and continue because, presumably, it suited most people most of the time: project staff felt they had developed something which met the needs of these pupils; project pupils had a strong sense of identity and also, in many cases, of achievement; non-project staff were happy that pupils with difficulties were in good hands. The only people who did not derive some benefit from the situation were those pupils who would have been selected for the project had it been able to accommodate more than 25 pupils per year and those who would have been selected on the former behavioural criteria. From time to time, concern surfaced over the unsatisfactory situation regarding the former group. Support teaching by subject staff was beginning to be organised, but as yet on a voluntary basis with no associated INSET or systematic procedures for diagnosing and monitoring individual learning difficulties of pupils. The support staff, whether 'remedial' or subject specialists, did not make as much use as they might have of the pupil records which came up from the middle school. Because these records were so variable, they were used mainly as a sorting device to help the head of intake year decide to which tutor group new pupils should be assigned. (Project staff had their own liaison with the middle schools.) To ease the timetabling of remedial teaching, all potential project pupils were identified at this stage and allocated to the same half year; in order to balance *the intake, the 'brighter' pupils were also allocated to this half year. In other words, the existence of project provision prospectively dominated the organisation of the third year. The risk of this was that if pupils were not identified as potential project pupils, they might miss out on help at a crucial stage. And if they were not in the event selected for the project, there was no special provision for them except what was on offer from teachers of bottom GCSE sets.*

At the same time, valuable developments which had taken place within the project - the increasingly sophisticated and formative use of profiling, practical and experiential learning, group work - were in effect not available to most non-project staff. This was so even when, as in the case of RoA pilot work in the school, the related work on project profiles would have been of immediate and practical use.

The unexpected catalyst for breaking down this structural inertia was the SMT's decision to reorganise the school's departmental structure into faculties, which would make for a closer relationship with the pastoral structure and for a leaner middle management team. A new role was envisaged for the school project leader, who would co-ordinate all support and special needs provision throughout the school, of which the project would now form only a part catering for half the number of pupils and for less time on the pupils' and project staff's weekly timetable.

Initially the proposals caused widespread consternation. Several staff felt that the changes had been announced, rather than discussed; because of falling pupil rolls and the impending effects of LMS, cuts in staffing were a part of the package. The fact that jobs were at stake was of more pressing concern to staff than the SMT's ostensible reasons for undertaking reorganisation at this time; a certain amount of anxiety and even distrust grew up. The school project leader was concerned that the project which had proved its worth was being dismantled without a guarantee that anything better would take its place. At the same time, he could see the argument for his having a wider, whole school brief. He also recognised the vulnerability of the project - its relatively generous staffing would be the first target when cuts had to be made, and open enrolment made it likely that the school would begin to place heavier emphasis on numbers taking public examinations; LMS might also mean that money for residentials, transport and other provision which characterised the project in its more 'enriched' form would become unavailable. Change was therefore inevitable, and, as we have seen, from many points of view desirable. The project leader and the SMT agreed that the issue in the short term was how to limit the damage; and in the longer term, how to build in a somewhat resistant environment, a whole school approach to the problems of low attainment. By the start of the following academic year, however, the SMT and project leader had worked through the issues to a point where a shared understanding and strategy had been reached.

Review: In Green Lane School it could be said that the project's signal success with 'its own' pupils both symptomised and perpetuated a problem within the school as a whole, which was the failure to allocate amongst all staff, or at least among all departments, the responsibility for identifying and tackling problems of low attainment wherever they occurred. This demonstrates the danger of assessing the success of an initiative purely in its own terms. A report by HMI on the LEA project (which followed a similar pattern in most schools) had been critical of its rigid framework and suggested that more pupils ought to be able to move more freely between the project and the mainstream (i.e. GCSE courses). This was too easily construed as a criticism of the alternative provision *per se* and seemed to project leaders and the central team not to take account of the real achievements of the pupils and the real advantages offered them. In our view, however, the weak link was actually the relationship between the initiative and the rest of the school. No one had really tackled the question of who had ownership of and/or responsibility for the project and what it stood for. There are good grounds for suggesting that, up until the reorganisation, the school had depended on the existence of the project to off-load difficult problems which a number of subject teachers had tended to ignore. And by the same token, however much project staff deplored the situation, the project had effectively depended on the lack of other systematic provision for low attainers in order to maintain its boundaries and hence its autonomy and flexibility. It says a good deal for the professional commitment of project leader and senior management that they had stood aside from entrenched, if defensible, positions to forge a common strategy to address these problems. By the end of our evaluation, an agreed and detailed course of action had been decided on. The project leader was taking the lead in setting out a coherent policy on support teaching for the whole school, which would also effectively end the marginalisation of 'the project'.

FAIRACRE

Sustaining and spreading the initiative in **Fairacre School** *did not present obvious problems if the 'outside world' stayed the same, though this was a period, of course, when the outside world was anything but stable. The most recent factor with a major bearing on the sustainability of its alternative course/accreditation scheme (developed and managed at county level) was the Secretary of State's review in the summer of 1989 of non-GCSE qualifications. The courses looked likely to continue for the time being, but in the light of national assessment proposals for the 16-plus age group, together with some uncertainty regarding the ultimate function of RoAs, the county team believed that the scheme's long-term significance lay in its principles rather than its system. That is to say, what mattered was its contribution to profiling techniques based on criterion referencing, to curriculum development and to teaching and learning strategies.*

This was on the face of it a promising way to approach the future. However, the operation of the initiative in Fairacre raised some questions about the feasibility of this, which are all the more pertinent given that the school had some dynamic and innovatory practices - in other words, it was a good example of the scheme and did not have overriding problems of its own. A relatively recent innovation, for example, was the lower school curriculum, designed around an integrated studies course, taught by form tutors and 'based on the best of primary practice in the area'; pupils were screened for literacy in their first year and provided with an individual literacy scheme. The emphasis on integration was continued into the upper school syllabuses, through the integrated humanities and integrated science courses, and the English and Communications (Information Technology) course. In keeping with this, TVEI had been introduced on the basis of its being available to all pupils. Another development was the introduction, starting in 1988 with the first year group, of a profiling system for recording pupils' achievement throughout their secondary school career. Special needs provision was organised, as might be expected on an integrated rather than a withdrawal model (though available only to pupils in years 1-3); support was being organised in design and manufacture, Information Technology, mathematics and English. The school was beginning to evolve the means to support gifted children as well.

Questions concerning the sustainability of the initiative then arose from a certain discrepancy between the initiative's philosophy (as expressed and practised by the LEA team) and the school's institutional structures and assumptions, rather than from any glaring deficiencies. To begin with, in contrast with the central team's reassurances, many staff described the scheme's profiling requirements as an 'administrative nightmare', taking up too much time in return for dubious gains. Procedures for moderating the pupils' work (involving attendance at half-day meetings centrally organised) were sometime side-stepped by one department in particular, whose head felt he could not spare staff for that amount of time given the various other demands which meant using supply cover. The timetable for notifying which students would be taking the course was disregarded by the same head of department, on the grounds that because they taught mixed ability groups, they could and should leave the decision of whether to enter individual pupils for GCSE or the county scheme open until the last minute. The head of another department was overtly critical of the 'instrumental' approach he believed had become dominant in his subject, and while making sure that the course guidelines were fulfilled by the time the pupils had reached the end of the fifth year, spent more time encouraging creative writing and reading the same texts as the GCSE groups than in 'form-filling and so-called life skills'. These staff were therefore able to give convincing reasons for their variance of procedural requirements. They were the ones who tended to encourage, indeed to insist on, a participatory and negotiated classroom style, which could also take the demands of profiling in its stride. Certainly pupils seemed to respond well in their lessons. But these particular teachers had many years' experience and expertise and the ensuing confidence to challenge accepted structures on the grounds of what they felt was best for pupils. Other, less experienced staff or teachers with less interest in developing their teaching strategies might never receive the support or challenge to offer a substantially different diet to low achievers from a rather undemanding 'bottom set' fare. If the traditional subject-based curriculum had already lost its meaning and appeal for these pupils (and there were signs that this was so), then the possibility of a few more certificates was not going to motivate them in itself. Links existed for professional development between subject teachers and the LEA team (either through regular procedures or if teachers requested individual help); between subject staff and their colleagues in the same department; and sometimes between subject teachers in neighbouring schools; but only by chance between subject staff in different departments of the same school who were teaching the same lower attaining pupils. The fact that the school co-ordinator was a deputy head, who was also clearly committed to staff development, undoubtedly gave status to the scheme, but might her senior position have inhibited teachers from asking for help when they most needed it?

So the growth points for the initiative (outlined above) seemed actually to be its weak points in terms of what could be guaranteed to happen in the school.

Review: The scenario in Fairacre School suggests that school planners need to consider what is involved in the relationship between the school and an externally developed initiative when the initiative in question has a strongly articulated philosophy and a system through which it is intended to operate, but where its implementation lies with individual departments and their teachers. Institutional practices in effect moulded the initiative, not vice versa. This is no doubt partly because whilst the initiative was certainly intended to encompass staff and curriculum development processes as well as assessment and accreditation procedures, the fact is that there were insufficient central (or school) resources to fulfil the staff development needs as more and more staff became involved. What is interesting is that despite the well articulated philosophy which was the moving force for the initiative, some teachers regarded its systems, procedures and course guidelines as its hallmark - that is, they awarded it a bureaucratic, rather than a pedagogical significance. This was particularly true of those senior teachers who had the expertise and confidence to take 'ownership' of the initiative, even by openly rejecting some of its procedural requirements, and thus, paradoxically, ensuring that educational needs, as they perceived them in their school, were given priority. There was a risk that the less experienced or confident teachers would, in observing the letter, be unable or unwilling to embody the spirit of the initiative.

SOME ISSUES FOR SCHOOL PLANNERS AND MANAGERS

At this point we would argue that the narratives and their accompanying reviews demonstrate the limitations of identifying and targeting a group or some groups of pupils for special treatment in ways which, in practice, treat the problem of lower attainment in isolation from the learning needs and difficulties of all pupils throughout their school careers.

We now would like to move on to a discussion of key issues which need to be considered in planning for differentiation.

**Issue
1:**

Are the objectives clear to everyone involved? Are there any hidden agendas or areas of obscurity?

We can see from the difficulties encountered in all four schools (Bankside, Broomhill, Green Lane and Fairacre) that a lack of clarity at certain critical points resulted in the impact of the initiative (in terms of benefits for particular pupils) being somewhat weakened and its potential (in terms of a wider influence) lessened. The fact that all four schools experienced problems shows how important it is to clarify all participants' roles and responsibilities. It further suggests that even if objectives are clear at the outset and strategy agreed on, unforeseen gaps in responsibilities or unintended effects of strategies may have to be dealt with. It cannot be assumed that once set in motion, the sheer momentum of the initiative will necessarily take it in the right direction.

As Michael Fullan has observed, 'Wherever you have more than one person with values, ideas and minds of their own, you have difficulties ... What distinguishes effective from ineffective administrators is not whether they can obliterate conflict, but how they anticipate it and deal with it as an inevitable and rational part of change and stability.' (*The Meaning of Educational Change*, Teachers College Press, New York, 1982, p. 162.)

Undoubtedly in some schools the prospect of any initiative involving greater differentiation focused upon the learning needs and difficulties of individual pupils is likely to encounter a mixed response from staff. Some will say that they are already doing it; some will welcome it conditionally; others will regard it unfavourably as yet another increase in their workload involving more time spent on assessment and less on what they regard as 'the real business of teaching'.

We found in our case study schools that the school management responded to lack of consensus and the prospect of the potential conflicts in a number of ways, all of which, we suspect, are fairly typical and each of which has its own potential risks and advantages.

One response is to seek to create a **bandwagon** on which all or most of the staff will eventually want to climb. Typically this was done either through a charismatic style of leadership where the forceful personality and dynamism of the head or another member of the SMT 'steers' the initiative or when responsibility for the initiative is given to a vanguard of committed teachers.

Both approaches often get results quickly, at least in the initial stages of the initiative, but charismatic leaders have a tendency to switch their energies from one innovation to another - sometimes before the groundwork has been laid for others to take the initiative on another stage. Charismatic managers are not necessarily the right people for ensuring that the initiative is consolidated and built up over a long period of time. The 'vanguard' also tends to enjoy early success but risks being marginalised by the rest of the staff, especially on an issue such as differentiation and particularly if the SMT does not sustain a high, and highly visible, level of support for the initiative and the team. There is also the risk that the team loses sight of how its operation dovetails with the rest of the school's curricular and organisational processes.

Generally speaking, then, a bandwagon effect may be a necessary condition for an initiative on differentiation to 'take off' in a school where there is some reluctance to adopt a change not just in policy but in practices, but it is seldom a sufficient condition to ensure success. There is also a need for long-term strategic planning; the 'doubters' have to be won round and persuaded that an initiative on differentiation ultimately affects all pupils and all staff indirectly and directly; that the proposed changes are not just rhetorical but also directed at classroom practice; some kind of monitoring and record-keeping system which has diagnostic value and yet is not over-bureaucratic will also need to be introduced; and, ultimately, a sense of participation in the planning and real understanding of the thinking behind the changes will have to be generated.

The second response which we observed - **management through consultation** - does indeed involve and engage staff in the planning as well as the implementation of the initiative and when it works it considerably increases the likelihood that the initiative will become incorporated into everyday classroom and school practice as well as policy. As a strategy it can also usefully complement attempts to create a bandwagon effect through charismatic leadership or a vanguard of teachers.

However, the consultative processes can be slow and time-consuming and during this phase there may be little progress to show for all the effort. Furthermore, it can never be assumed that consultation will automatically lead to consensus - it may instead bring to the surface latent tensions and disagreements and polarise the staff.

The third typical response to the problem identified by Fullan is what we would describe as **'the softly softly style of management'.** It recognises the likelihood of resistance among staff to a particular change and seeks to circumvent this by a gradual introduction of change. The risk, however, is that it might forfeit a wider understanding among staff of what is being done and inhibit the pace of change to the point where it falters altogether. In the meantime, the more innovative become frustrated at the slowness of the change and those opposed to it become equally concerned that too much is happening too quickly. Before long, conspiracy theories abound in the staffroom and a lot of work has to be done to recreate a 'climate' that will engender any kind of change.

We shall return to some of the problems outlined here later in the text, but at this point it is worth noting that in two of our case study schools they have independently come up with the idea of **contracts** which specify the school's objectives and strategies for the initiative, and clarify the extent and role of advisory input from the LEA team. Such a contract could perhaps be integrated with a school's development plan. The principle need not be limited to initiatives which require LEA input, nor need it have legalistic connotations - it might amount to the explicit and agreed formulation of a whole school strategy (see the following section).

Again, our four schools each showed a tendency to compound these categories, which suggests this is a common problem. Staff in some schools (such as Little Stoke) have acted as **teacher-researchers,** keeping a journal of classroom activities for self-review and discussion with colleagues. Whilst this is a time-consuming and even to some staff a slightly threatening exercise, it can be a valuable contribution to an overall in-school evaluation of an initiative. But it also needs a **management perspective** which will look at the dynamic relationship between what is being done through the initiative and what is being done in the rest of the school.

Planners in schools like Green Lane, for example, moving towards integrating the project with provision in the rest of the school, will need to identify how the project has achieved benefits for its pupils and to explore the possibilities of replicating those conditions, procedures and provision in a non-project environment. Another school in the same authority has developed an intermediate model of provision, which allows some pupils to take a few GCSEs, with the project staff providing support in the pupils' non-subject periods. Such a model makes it possible for selected pupils to opt into examined syllabuses, though mechanisms for enabling other pupils to 'drop out' of some of their GCSEs into this more supported framework need further exploration. The situation in Broomhill School, in another authority, underlines this need.

The need to identify an initiative's strengths and weaknesses also arises when more radical change is mooted. The county in which The King's School is situated ran a pilot programme with eight schools (The King's School did not participate at this stage) which provided a curriculum package for 14-16 year old low attainers, accredited by a county award. At the end of this pilot stage, however, the county team decided to redirect LAPP resources towards 'differentiating' the curriculum for the whole 11-16 age range. In one of the pilot schools, where the

Issue 2:

What are the strengths and weaknesses of the initiative in curricular, organisational and resourcing terms? Can they be separated out in practice so that it is the positive innovations and not merely the organisational advantages which are taken forward?

14-16 curriculum package was still extant albeit in attenuated form, some curriculum differentiation work for third years was being undertaken by a junior member of the humanities department, under the guidance of a former member of the advisory team. This work had great potential, but it looked as if any messages from the original 14-16 package were being lost in the process. It was in danger of being marginalised without any systematic whole school appraisal of how its objectives and strategies might be relevant to the new initiative.

Again, this is a common, if sometimes unrecognised, issue, usually becoming manifest as the initiative moves from implementation to institutionalisation. It is often a question of a hiatus in responsibility, where it is pretty clear whose duty it is to run the initiative on a day-to-day basis - planning, organising and teaching the curriculum, arranging meetings among participating staff, preparing reports and documents for school management, school colleagues and LEA personnel, identifying individual staff development needs - but unclear as to who should be making strategic decisions regarding the objectives of the initiative in so far as they relate to whole school provision. It may be that in practice 'ownership' is fragmented among different groups of people: project leaders, teaching staff, school managers, LEA advisors are the most obvious groups. Clearly, they are almost bound to have contrasting, even incompatible, perspectives on how the initiative should be developed, which come into the open when one party decides that changes need to be made, as in Green Lane; or which can be discussed only as the implications of taking a particular direction become clear, as in Broomhill. Or school managers may act as if 'ownership' lies with all teachers designated as participants, whereas some teachers operate in the passive resistance mode, as they did in Bankside. There is clearly a tension between the need on the one hand for a particular group to have '*ownership*' of an initiative - in the sense of a commitment to its principle, the *incentive* to make it work, the '*viability*' which will assist and encourage colleagues to become involved and the *accountability* for its successes and failures - and on the other for the initiative to be *accessible* to the whole school, both conceptually and operationally. The resolution of this tension, this shift from implementation to institutionalisation, appears to be one of the most delicate tasks demanded of school managers.

Our schools give us different models of the processes and problems involved, though it might be said that Green Lane and Fairacre took institutionalisation rather for granted and made no distinct provision for it as a different kind of process. Two instructive models in this context are:

Reliance on a vanguard of teachers. Managers in both Broomhill and Bankside, though in different ways and for different reasons, assumed a vanguard of teachers was the way to carry forward the intended changes. The situation in Bankside highlights a fairly common managerial dilemma when the initiative is primarily concerned with a major change in teaching styles and practice. Some

Issue 3:

Where does 'ownership' of the initiative actually lie? What implications does this have for sustaining it and for spreading it?

Issue 4:

Is the strategy used for initiating and implementing the innovation therefore the most effective one for institutionalising and/or spreading it?

teachers were more committed or more successful than others when it came to working with colleagues to develop integrated teaching materials. In subsequent years, as the head and SMT sought to involve more and more staff in the integrated curriculum approach, the 'softly softly' strategy outlined above helped to paper over some of the cracks between staff regarding the value of curriculum integration. It also meant that some staff, although timetabled to integrate with their colleagues, felt no great compulsion to participate. School-based INSET might have helped to engender a wide-scale reappraisal of existing practices, but the problem here was that most of the successful 'integrators' were on MPG and most of the vociferous critics of integration were heads of year or heads of department and unwilling to be 'told how to teach' by colleagues who were less experienced. It seems to have been one of those situations where the conventional management strategy of a pilot phase involving a few teachers followed by an extension programme intended gradually to win over and then involve all staff is likely to encounter problems. There seems to a strong case here for the implementation process to be preceded by (rather than leading to) a process of whole staff discussions, consciousness-raising and large-scale consultation.

Setting up phased inter-departmental working parties. The head of Little Stoke School introduced each new initiative, including oracy work, to the school on a similar model. An inter-departmental working group was set up, which consisted of a few teachers who had shown an interest in the initiative and whose commitment and drive would 'get it off the ground'. Out of this emerged two further stages of institutionalisation, a development group followed by a standing committee. It was likely, and probably desirable, that some of the people in the working party would form the core of the development group, but less likely or desirable, that they should go on to become the standing committee. This last stage should include some senior and middle management staff, whereas the earlier stages might well be better steered by more junior staff. This would seem to be a recognition by the head that the embedding and dissemination of an initiative may call for different skills from those required for its initial development and above all, for greater political clout. It was noticeable that at this stage - the development group stage - staff from each of the major departments, apart from humanities, had become involved in oracy work on a volunteer basis. But they tended not to be senior staff; and though their commitment to different ways of working (such as non-directive teaching and active learning as well as the encouragement of oral expression) was conspicuous, it was less clear that they all shared the same conception of the 'oracy' initiative either as an end in itself or as a means to other educational ends. Nor was it evident that they had been able to get their departmental colleagues actively involved. Some other means of defining a policy for, and then systematically spreading, oracy work throughout the school was clearly called for; and though it was too early to assess the outcome in this case, the strategy adopted by the head seems promising.

Most initiatives reach a potential impasse at some stage, because of personnel or structures or earlier decisions. We have indicated above how one or two forms of what one might call systemic resistance might be overcome. But it is striking how changes in one part or aspect of school provision seem to call for changes in other areas. Our schools have all been aware of such needs; perhaps the most relevant areas where some level of rethinking has taken place have been:

Redefinition of project staff roles. The expertise project staff are likely to have developed over the course of implementing and managing an innovation is a crucial resource for colleagues. But as the case of Green Lane shows, the more autonomous and 'bounded' the initiative, the less easy it is for this expertise to be made available for colleagues in addressing the needs of low attaining pupils. The school project leader's change of role to encompass a much wider brief is intended to address this problem, even though there is an attendant risk that he or she will be able to devote less energy to overseeing the project. By contrast, the model for introducing initiatives in Little Stoke meant that project teachers would after a while shed their project role and revert to their previous responsibilities, but taking with them the expertise they had gained from participating in the project.

In Fairacre, as more subject-based alternative courses became available and it was clear that the initiative had in one important sense become self-sustaining, more and more teachers found themselves teaching such courses. Teachers became 'project' staff only as and when they taught the alternative courses, which might change each year according to departmental practice and/or timetable arrangements and might involve an individual teacher in all or only some of the total periods per week with a class. There was thus the possibility for most staff to become conversant with the principles and practice of the initiative, but the decision was a pragmatic one and meant that related staff development was patchy and *ad hoc,* with staff in different departments not often having the chance to learn from each other. Similarly in Bankside, as the head sought deliberately to involve more teachers in the initiative, some expertise was lost by the original project teachers not being either timetabled to teach the integrated curriculum in the following year or else given explicit responsibility for helping to develop their colleagues' expertise.

The King's School, in changing from a remedial to a whole school model of individual pupil support, had in practice to create a new post. This change was facilitated by the fact that the former special needs teacher had left and the gap had been filled temporarily by a member of the senior management team. The need to appoint a new member of staff was easily combined with the opportunity to create a new philosophy of pupil support.

Issue 5:

Is it possible to identify at what points the 'spread' of the innovation is likely to be impeded?

Redeployment of special needs provision. The change from a 'remedial' model to a pupil support model - now increasingly common in school, at least rhetorically - involves changes in the role of the special needs staff. It also requires changes in their own and others' perceptions of their potential contribution to identifying and addressing individual pupils' learning needs and problems, whether those pupils are part of some defined group or not. As we have seen, The King's School was already exploring the possibility of a much wider role for the special needs co-ordinator than had previously been the case (and with the active encouragement of LEA policy); other schools, while not going so far in a single step, were also rethinking special needs provision. Fairacre and Green Lane were instituting subject specialist in-class support on a timetabled and a voluntary basis respectively. There were initial problems with this, such as the difficulty of reaching a practicable working definition of what 'support teaching' meant, and how best to record, co-ordinate and put to use information on individual pupils. But perhaps the issue that most needs highlighting is how to change ingrained perceptions of what the special needs staff are there to do; clearly, whole school pupil support cannot be undertaken on an individual pupil basis by 2.5 staff. The shift from working solely or mainly with 'statemented' pupils to co-ordinating pupil support provision for the whole school involved two major changes of perception: first, towards the involvement of special needs staff in staff development, and a corresponding shift towards subject specialist and pastoral roles being expanded to encompass greater responsibility for diagnosing and addressing the learning needs of pupils throughout their school career. This has implications for the current tendency to allocate special needs provision to the lower school (years 1-3) and thus to perpetuate a split between upper and lower curricula provision.

Second, it requires a change in the formal status and in other people's perceptions of special needs staff. For example, in more than one school we heard the view expressed of special needs teachers as: 'low status kids, low status teachers' and even 'thick kids, thick teachers'. One of the contributions LAPP made was to enhance the career prospects of staff engaged in teaching lower ability pupils. It may be that the introduction of the National Curriculum will impel a general widening of the special needs brief which we have begun to see already as schools are faced with the necessity of teaching ten foundation subjects to pupils of all abilities. The move to incorporate the needs of gifted children in special needs work must also enhance its status.

Finally, are school managers sufficiently aware of what special needs staff can offer their specialist colleagues (identifying reading ages of pupils, reading levels of texts, familiarity with suitable teaching strategies and materials, etc.)? Are they sufficiently aware of the developmental role special needs staff can play in the school (supporting staff in a team-teaching context, co-ordinating different kinds of pupil support, liaising on a regular basis between academic and pastoral sectors and with outside agencies). And is there not some truth in the idea that the existence of remedial provision actually de-skills subject teachers?

A coherent programme of INSET. The developments in **City Road Comprehensive** are dealt with in more detail in the following section, but some of the problems identified in Bankside and Broomhill emerged in this school too, and it is worth focusing here on how the school sought to deal with them. Initially, the teachers responsible for the project had been given a fairly free hand to develop the initiative with little input from the SMT or from the staff as a whole. It was only once they reached the implementation stage that major differences of interpretation emerged between the head and the team and between the team and the staff. These differences were not so much about the worth of the innovation *per se*, but about its priority and place within the broader development strategy of the school. In response to this, the head took a more pro-active role, holding planning meetings with the team for half a day a week every week, and they in turn initiated a rolling programme of staff consultation and planning not only to raise consciousness but also to generate commitment to the implementation of the initiative.

Here we would merely draw your attention to the fact that two LEA teams, on the basis of pilot work with schools rethought their initiatives from scratch and moved away from a pupil-oriented approach to a teacher-oriented one. That is to say, they recognised that in order for pupils to change, teachers had to change their assumptions, their perceptions and their practices. But they were also beginning to recognise that for grass-roots approaches with teachers to result in lasting change within an institution, management policies and organisational structures must change to support them.

This is the issue at the heart of the following, final section. It concerns the tension between the need for an initiative on the problems of low attainment to be taken up throughout the school (all staff and all pupils all the time) if it is to have a lasting and effective impact; and the need to keep concern for the most vulnerable pupils in the foreground. The most 'dispersed' kinds of provision, such as oracy, integrated curricula and curriculum differentiation were the ones likely to generate a high level of acceptance of the initiative's principles from most staff; perhaps they were also at most risk of subsuming the needs of individual low attaining pupils to the needs of the group.

To sum up: we have seen signs in some schools of attempts to introduce **change across the whole age and ability range.** This often involves making use of more than one kind of provision, whether targeted or dispersed. It also requires long term strategic thinking on the part of school planners, and this has caused problems in some schools for a variety - or combination - of reasons. For example, because the planners themselves had not done that thinking at the appropriate

Issue 6:

What, if any, indications are there that priorities and/or focus need to be re-appraised and a different approach tried?

Issue 7:

How can the interests of low attainers continue to be safeguarded as an initiative becomes institutionalised

S E C T I O N 4

throughout the structures and systems of the school?

time, but had tended instead to be reactive to circumstances or to prioritise organisational issues at the expense of curricular ones; or because there was an enduring resistance to change among key staff (often for quite understandable reasons); or because external pressure (such as falling rolls or teacher shortages) made it next to impossible to devise a coherent long-term plan.

The implementation of the National Curriculum, together with the implications of local management, have been impelling school planners to take a **more unified approach to school development** (which has its legalistic expression in the school development plan). Sometimes the motivation for this has been defensive - that is, undertaken out of a need to preserve continuity (whether of staffing and structures or of curricular initiatives instigated and resourced before the 1988 Education Act). But sometimes the drive towards greater coherence has come from schools' determination that if changes have to be made, they should stimulate and co-ordinate rather than suppress or fragment their recent and partial innovations in such areas as formative assessment, integration of the curriculum, negotiated learning and review, teaching strategies which facilitate pupils' own learning and so forth. In the following section, TOWARDS A WHOLE SCHOOL STRATEGY FOR RAISING ATTAINMENT, we examine the possibilities for creating a whole school strategy in the context of what can currently be predicted about the implications of the National Curriculum and Local Management of Schools.

Meanwhile, if we refer back to the discussion of targeting and dispersion in Section 3, it becomes apparent that in a whole school context, **targeted provision** can play a crucial transitional role - as is still the case, for example, in Green Lane and The King's School. Moreover, for a number of reasons, distinct provision for groups of pupils will probably need to continue alongside the development of a whole school approach. This discussion is taken up in the following section. **Dispersed provision**, on the other hand, can act as a lever for the uneven but continuous process of whole school change, as in the cases of City Road Comprehensive and Little Stoke. If groups of teachers within and across departments have been tackling information and management systems in new ways, or modifying parts of the curriculum for different year groups or teaching strategies or their own roles and responsibilities, the school will already be 'primed' for change on a broad front. It should be noted, though, that the degree of dispersion - provision apparently implemented throughout a number of different subject or organisational areas in the school - does not necessarily indicate the depth of its impact on a school, as the cases of Bankside and Little Stoke illustrate.

*T*OWARDS
A
WHOLE
SCHOOL
STRATEGY
FOR
RAISING
ATTAINMENT

SUMMARY OF THE ARGUMENT SO FAR

Before embarking on the main focus of this section this wo͟͟ ͟͟ ͟͟ an appropriate point to review the key issues and lessons about differentiation which have emerged in earlier sections:

Differentiation is a key issue in any consideration of the processes of curriculum change and planning. It usually manifests itself in one of two broad forms: **differentiation between groups** and **differentiation between individual pupils** - although these are not necessarily mutually exclusive.

Organisational priorities often play a more significant role in identifying 'lower attainers' than the individual learning needs and difficulties of the pupils.

As a result, in most schools **some pupils' needs are not being adequately met.**

But in practice lower attainers are not an homogeneous group within the school and consequently any attempt to respond to their needs in a uniform way is likely to have a limited effect. Rather than focus on 'the problem of lower attainers' it makes more sense to think in terms of **the problems of lower attainment.**

Different kinds of learning problems brought about by different factors call for **differentiated responses** by the school.

Some of the learning needs and problems identified in 14-16 year olds can be traced back to primary and early secondary education. Consequently **responses at 14 tend to be 'holding devices'** or ways of containing the problem rather than solutions.

Therefore, unless **changes lower down the school** are also initiated, the problems are likely to recur in every subsequent generation of young school leavers.

Differentiated responses presuppose an **effective system of identifying pupils' learning needs and problems.**

For every problem there is a **variety of curriculum and organisational solutions.** Some focus on a distinct aspect of provision, other address changes in the whole system.

The main task is to find **a range of solutions** which meet the diversity of pupils' learning needs yet are **appropriate to the school,** bearing in mind its structure and organisation, the resources available, the preparedness of staff and the likely barriers to change.

The different solutions adopted need to be systematically **monitored and reappraised** over time:

(a) to see if they are achieving what they are supposed to;

(b) to gauge the actual progress being made by learners;

(c) to identify their strengths, weaknesses and future implications in curricular, organisational and resourcing terms;

(d) to assess subsequent priorities in the light of the changes which have already taken place.

The structured and organisational arrangements introduced to meet the diversity of learning needs and difficulties of pupils **needs to be flexible** since the range and distribution of pupils' needs can vary considerably with each new intake.

The management strategies and the people employed to set up and implement innovative changes may not necessarily be the most appropriate or the most effective ones for:

(a) ensuring its **successful institutionalisation** within the school; or

(b) **dissemination** of the new ideas and practices to all staff (e.g. the qualities required for a successful innovator are not always the qualities needed for an effective manager or disseminator).

Long-term planning is usually important in implementing, institutionalising and incorporating any major change in a school. It **is essential when the changes are designed to differentiate between individual pupils** rather than between groups because it has long-term implications for staffing, staff development, management structures and inter-departmental co-operation. Inevitably, however, this kind of planning is particularly vulnerable to changing circumstances (falling rolls, teacher shortages, the curricular and organisational implications of the 1988 Education Act).

WHAT GENERAL IMPLICATIONS CAN BE DRAWN FOR WHOLE SCHOOL PLANNING?

- A coherent plan needs to be drawn up that will initiate changes which address the needs of the whole age range and not just the 14-16 school population, and the needs of all pupils and not just the least able.

- Devising a whole school plan and convincing all the staff of its potential advantages over the existing arrangements will be difficult enough; ensuring that it will be sufficiently responsive and adaptable to major changes in the pipeline (Local Management of Schools, National Curriculum, attainment target testing, open enrolment, demographic changes etc.) and unforeseen changes is even more problematical.

- It should be clear by now that the very diversity of pupils' learning needs and difficulties necessitates some kind of differentiated approach. But the emphasis, we would argue, should be on differentiation as a **pedagogical principle** - how best to cater for the complex multiplicity of needs of individuals - rather than differentiation as an **organisational strategy -** a means of grouping pupils with apparently similar needs and abilities and then tailoring the content, methods and pace of their learning to the assumed level of the group.

- Changes on this scale cannot be introduced overnight. They call for a long-term strategy. In the meantime the problems facing the 14-16 year olds likely to drop out or do poorly in GCSEs remain. So an effective whole school strategy for raising attainment needs to combine long-term remedies with short-term or interim solutions to more immediate and pressing problems.

WHAT IS A WHOLE SCHOOL STRATEGY?

The notion of a whole school policy only really came into common currency after the publication of the Bullock Report (DES, 1975). But, to date, it has tended to be associated almost exclusively with specific themes and areas such as equal opportunities, multi-cultural education, special needs and language. More recently the notion of an overarching whole school strategy has come into use as a means of achieving whole school policies.

So what do we mean by a whole school strategy for raising attainment? We would argue that it has four key elements:

One which involves all or most teachers

- which breaks down the barriers between pastoral and academic;

- which encourages members of departments to take a less parochial view of their subject area;

- which involves more staff in key decisions;

- which thereby encourages a sense of ownership not just of their own teaching but of the school's curriculum as a whole.

One which reviews the whole curriculum of all pupils (11-16) and establishes effective procedures for ensuring continuity and progression

In most schools the only people who know the whole curriculum are the pupils, and their knowledge is still partial. Without some kind of curriculum review or mapping exercise, whole school change is simply not feasible.

One which takes full account of the pupils pre-secondary experience (5-11/8-13)

- how much use is made of the intake's primary or middle school records? How is the information co-ordinated? How is it actually used?

- curriculum review (11-16) may also require a mapping of what pupils did in primary or middle schools to effect a smoother and more economical transition to secondary.

One which responds to the different and changing needs of each pupil

- when needs are identified and made known to all staff who need to know;

- where the response is flexible to changing needs and circumstances;

- where the responses to chronological needs are monitored across the pupil's curriculum.

At this point, staff in most schools would probably say: this is all very well, but in our school decisions about these issues are usually determined by prior decisions concerning the organisation of the school, such as staffing, pastoral structures, academic structures, timetable arrangements, financial resources, staff development and support procedures. This was certainly true of our case study schools, and that is precisely why many projects became marginalised within schools, particularly as the external funding was phased out.

The reason why decisions about innovation appear to be determined primarily by organisational constraints is that in many schools the decision-makers have a clearer notion of, and better information about, what these entail. Hence the importance of a comprehensive curriculum review before embarking on whole school change. It is also our hope and intention that the process of working through this Handbook should have made at least some of those innovative decisions more amenable to this kind of analysis.

Diagram 4

The LAP Programme did not produce a universal blueprint for raising attainment but the initiative has made it possible to identify a series of questions that need to be asked before an effective whole school strategy for raising attainment can be developed and implemented. The questions have been grouped into four distinct processes which together form a cycle of change for the development of whole school strategies. We realise, however, that schools may well be at different stages in that cyclical

process; many will have conducted a comprehensive cu[...]
the last year or so; some may now be using training da[...]
implications of that review; some may have begun to plan [...]
changes.

It is possible therefore to regard this battery of questions as either a useful starting point before embarking on the development of a whole school strategy or as a checklist for reviewing decisions already taken.

Mapping the territory

1. **What is currently being done about the problems of 'lower attainment'?**

    -   within the curriculum
    -   in terms of pupil groupings
    -   in terms of pastoral approach
    -   in terms of special needs provision
    -   through monitoring pupils' needs and progress
    -   in terms of staff development and changing pedagogy.

Challenging assumptions

2. **What does this tell you about how your school interprets the problems?**

    -   what assumptions are being made about pupils?
    -   how widely shared amongst staff are these assumptions?
    -   how extensive is the problem assumed to be?

3. **Can the assumptions implicit in this interpretation be substantiated?**

    -   what is being done to collect information in order to diagnose pupils' needs?
    -   how accessible is the information?
    -   who co-ordinates it?
    -   is the information being used and how?

4. **Are the diverse needs of all pupils being adequately met? How do you know?**

    -   who, if anyone, has responsibility for tracking an individual pupil's curriculum throughout any particular year and throughout her or his school life?

- are there any new developments in the role, remit and day-to-day practices of the special needs co-ordinator?

- how are individual pupils' learning needs, problems and aptitudes diagnosed, monitored and addressed? What sort of record collection, retrieval and transfer system exists within the school and how does it operate?

- how is achievement assessed and recorded? Are there major differences of approach between departments?

5. **What scope is there for improvement?**

- what are the major constraints on change?

- what are the chances of overcoming them?

- to what extent can those involved in curriculum planning make use of the information held on individual pupils?

Planning the change

6. **What would be your priorities?**

- Whole school change is a long-term process. As one head teacher described it, 'it's a painful process of two steps forward and one step back'. Some argue for initiating change with first year pupils and allowing it to work its way through the school. But in the meanwhile there may be a need for   short-term initiatives to deal with the most pressing problems, such as pupils dropping out from GCSE.

7. **What needs to be done in order to move from 'containing' the problems of lower attainers to raising attainment for all? What changes are needed in terms of:**

- curriculum 14-16?

- curriculum pre-14?

- transition from primary/middle to secondary?

- pupil groupings throughout the school?

- the pastoral system?

- special needs provision?

- staff development?

- procedures for diagnosing individual needs and learning difficulties?

- procedures for monitoring and assessing progress?

- teaching styles?

- use of individualised learning schemes?

8. **What is a realistic timetable for implementing the proposed changes?**

- what can you realistically hope to achieve in the first year?

- what short-term or interim measures will be necessary?

- how long will it take to effectively implement all the changes you are proposing?

- what innovations or changes will need to be permanently monitored and by whom?

9. **Is the existing organisational framework appropriate?**

- is the existing structure for curriculum planning adequate for the task?

- how can the whole staff be given responsibility for and/or ownership of the process?

- are the lower and upper school curricula to be integrated into a coherent three/five year process?

10. **Will the changes you want to institute:**

- be flexible enough to meet the range of learning problems you have identified with the current intake?

- be responsive enough to incoming populations of pupils who may vary in terms of the range and extent of their learning needs and difficulties from the current school population?

11. **Are the proposed changes robust enough to withstand future changes in staffing?**

12. **Are the proposed short-term strategies and changes compatible with the proposed long-term ones?**

13. **What needs to be done to explain the changes and promote support for them amongst:**

- the whole staff?

- school governors?

- all pupils?

- all parents?

Making it happen

Some of our case study schools have now moved toward the development of their own whole school strategies for raising attainment. We conclude this section of the Handbook, therefore, with some further narrative material on their progress. For background to two of the schools, **Robinswood High** and **City Road Comprehensive**, you may like to refer back to the earlier portraits of schools on pages 18-19 in Section 1, pages 43 - 44 in Section 3, and page 64 in Section 4. The third school, **Tweedmill**, has not been discussed in any detail elsewhere, but is included here because of its particular approach for involving all staff in diagnosing and responding to underachievement throughout the age and ability range.

ROBINSWOOD

*It was noted earlier (page 18) that from the outset **Robinswood High School** intentionally avoided treating lower attainers as a distinct and homogeneous target group requiring an alternative curriculum. Three years into the project they embarked on a second phase of consolidating or institutionalising the initiative. A cross-curricular team was set up, with its own co-ordinator and with full support from the SMT, to co-ordinate a range of cross-curricular initiatives and generally to operate as a kind of whole school curriculum development agency. The team proposed a way of restructuring the curriculum and the timetable to facilitate the introduction of some modular courses and specific initiatives in special needs, Information Technology, Records of Achievement, etc. A year later the head introduced a new and more flexible management structure to support this work. Five interrelated management groups have been set up, four of which involve all members of staff:*

❏ *Senior Management Team (head, three deputy heads and two assistant heads)*

❏ *Five development teams (Resources, Curriculum, Community, Assessment, Staff Development) led by the deputies and assistant heads;*

❏ *Six faculty teams led by co-ordinators for language and communications, mathematics, science, creative arts, recreational studies and the humanities (involving all the staff in each faculty);*

❏ *Six cross-curricular teams covering Information Technology, PSE, active learning, equal opportunities, special needs and the use of the community as a resource for learning;*

❏ *Six year teams led by heads of year which form the basis of a horizontally -organised pastoral care and guidance system built upon mixed ability form groups.*

All staff are members of at least four kinds of planning team and therefore have an opportunity to shape policy and, above all, to scrutinise any curriculum or policy change from all four distinct perspectives. The head estimates that it will probably take at least five years to achieve what they are setting out to do, i.e. to promote the effective delivery of a relevant, broad and balanced curriculum, which provides for coherence and progression, and recognises individual pupils' diverse learning needs.

Review: The style of management approximates to what we described in Section 4 as consultative in that it maximises the opportunities for all staff to participate in the planning and implementation of the whole school strategy. But it assumes that this process will lead to consensus about the direction and worth of change. The opposite - increased polarisation within the staff - could just as easily emerge out of the process. Involving all staff at different levels of planning (e.g. development teams, faculties, cross-curricular teams and year teams) has the advantage of ensuring that each individual member of staff views the whole school strategy from more than just his or her personal standpoint as a classroom teacher, head of department or member of SMT. If polarisation does emerge and yet the SMT continues to remain committed to consultation then there may well be a lengthy period of negotiation before evidence of practical changes becomes apparent. The alternative would be for SMT to be more directive and risk losing the support of those innovators who have appreciated the opportunity to contribute to the process of change. In terms of the cycle of change, Robinswood is well into the process of planning but it is too soon to judge the impact of these proposed and implemented changes. The means have been put in place for delivering staff change and organisational change, but ultimately the 'proof of the pudding' lies in whether the reorganisation can deliver change for the pupils, and this has to take place at a time when other changes - LMS, National Curriculum and testing, open enrolment, reductions in staffing, and changes in teachers pay and conditions of service - create their own agenda for change which cannot be ignored.

CITY ROAD

City Road Comprehensive, with its pupil roll down to 350, found itself in a situation which, though unfavourable on many counts (widespread underachievement, apathy and low expectations among pupils, high social deprivation in the area and the threat of closure) was undoubtedly well-suited to whole school change. The rationale underpinning the changes can be summarised as follows. Although many of the pupils come to the school with a history of low attainment, poor motivation and low expectations, their 'symptoms' of lower attainment were being reinforced by what was essentially a traditional 'secondary modern curriculum': rigid patterns of teacher specialisation, little interaction between departments, traditional teaching methods and unrelated pastoral and curricular systems. The SMT felt that there was a need to:

- *reduce 'curriculum clutter'*
- *break down subject barriers*

- *create more stable relationships between staff and pupils*
- *integrate special needs provision*
- *create more opportunities for individually-paced and negotiated learning*
- *integrate the pastoral and the academic*
- *improve the transition from primary to secondary.*

Changes of this magnitude called for not only a curriculum review but also an organisational review. The outcomes of this were:

- *the time allocated for the common core in upper school was extended, and the time available and range of choice for options was reduced;*

- *the role of form teachers was enhanced by allocating 18 per cent of the week to PSE, guidance and counselling between form teachers and their forms;*

- *cross-curricular teams were set up to look at the scope for integration across subject boundaries and for promoting cross-curricular themes such as language and communication, Information Technology;*

- *to assist transition from primary to secondary the school has introduced a kind of base tutor system where first year pupils spend a large proportion of the week with one teacher.*

The implementation of these changes was facilitated to some degree by the LEA's staff secondment programme which freed key staff to engage in curriculum planning and development work and the school's own INSET programme for developing new skills, e.g. in counselling.

Review: **City Road** is a good example of a school gradually coming to the realisation that the problems of lower attainment within the school are increasing with each new intake and are not going to be effectively combated by a series of discrete initiatives. The management strategy adopted initially had been delegatory - a group of committed teachers fired with enthusiasm for innovation through their secondments and being given their head to put their ideas in practice. The curricular and organisational reviews, however, revealed the need for more coherent and co-ordinated change. As a result the school's SMT took a more directive role, and a number of structural and organisational changes were introduced.

The school now finds itself entering the 'Making it Happen' phase and the issues emerging relate to how to convince pupils and parents of the value of the changes being introduced and how best to explain their purpose (e.g. the introduction of primary school practice is clashing with some pupils' expectations of what secondary schooling is all about). The school is exploring whether pupils and parents are receiving adequate information about the learning needs of the intake year; how best to develop greater curricular coherence from lower to upper school; and how to deliver the National Curriculum through the curriculum structure which is emerging.

TWEEDMILL

Tweedmill, a county town comprehensive with just under 1,000 pupils, was initially a LAPP associate school and only became a full project school in 1986. The school has adopted many of the features of the LEA's LAPP approach - school-community links, residentials, provision for developing thinking skills - and the mainstream curriculum has traditionally included a number of 'carousel courses'. The head of special needs had used a half-time secondment (a benefit of the school's participation in the LEA LAPP follow-up) to carry out an extensive inquiry into underachievement across the ability range. This has included interviewing all staff teaching the third year and a number of pupils. Teachers have been enabled to articulate the criteria they use, and it has become clear that underachievement can often go undetected because teachers don't have the opportunity to get to know pupils well enough, partly because 'carousel' courses mean frequent changes of teacher and partly because information does not get passed around from teacher to teacher. The head of special needs has now been put in charge of PSE and is using this as an opportunity to work towards a whole school strategy intended to change how teachers work with pupils. A believer in the efficacy of teams in bringing about change, he hopes gradually to put together a strong PSE team and tutor teams as a way of transforming the now established RoA reporting system into a continuing and ever more effective strategy of recording and reviewing achievement as it happens across the curriculum. The year tutors, it is hoped, will be key features in setting a new style and approach with pupils.

Review: Although **Tweedmill** is not as advanced in the cycle of change as **Robinswood** and **City Road** it represents an interesting alternative. Rather than start by conducting a curricular or organisational review they have 'mapped the territory' in terms of the criteria used by all staff for identifying the low attainment and underachievement of individual pupils. Also it is fairly unusual in LAPP terms for the management of change to be in the hands of the head of special needs.

The management structure is similar to the one we labelled 'softly softly' in Section 4, through a 'vanguard' of innovators - the PSE team and year tutors. However, the ultimate success or failure of the strategy will be in all staff adopting the same criteria and procedures for identifying and responding to underachievement and the experience of many other project schools suggests that it is often difficult to effect the necessary 'jump' from vanguard to whole school innovations, especially when that vanguard is located in the pastoral care system and not the academic structure.

DIFFERENTIATION IN THE NINETIES

Within the last ten years many of the most innovative approaches to differentiation have emerged in the 14-16 curriculum - often supported and encouraged by initiatives such as LAPP, TVEI and RoAs - and in the intake year of secondary education (both in 11-18 and 13-18 schools).

In the main, these innovative approaches have evolved to cope with specific problems in schools:

- the provision of more effective and relevant learning experiences for young people who otherwise might leave school after eleven years of compulsory education with little to show for it;

- a smoother transition from primary or middle to secondary.

However, a number of current and emerging issues, many of which arise directly out of the Education Acts of 1981, 1986 and 1988 and subsequent statements by Education Ministers, will have implications for differentiation in schools in the 1990s. We are thinking, for example, of such issues and concerns as:

- the delivery of the **National Curriculum** (in discrete subjects, inter-disciplinary, cross-curricular, etc.);

- the possible impact of **attainment targets** and **programmes of study** on teaching approaches and pupil groupings;

- the **summative/formative debate** concerning the nature and purpose of SATs;

- the possible effects of the above changes on the time teachers will have to **diagnose** individual pupil's learning needs and difficulties;

- the possible effect of **open enrolment** on some small inner city schools which already have pupil intakes heavily skewed towards the lower end of the ability range;

- **teacher shortages** in key areas of the curriculum;

- the implications of **Local Management in Schools** for resourcing, staffing and staff development, and the possible constraints of formula funding on some schools' ability to provide a broad, balanced and differentiated curriculum;

- the long-term viability and value of those **alternative forms of assessment, recording and accreditation** which emerged in the mid-1980s.

Some of these issues will provide new challenges for current thinking and practices with regard to differentiation, but others could reinforce many of the assumptions and practices we have been questioning in this Handbook.

What is certain is that most of the changes which education is now undergoing will not *in themselves* do anything to diminish the problems of lower attainment. The need for a whole school strategy for raising attainment remains of paramount importance.

AGENDA

F O R

I N S E T

We offer here a number of staff development activities that school planners could use with particular planning teams (e.g. heads of department, curriculum working parties, cross-curricular teams, etc.), or strategically important departments (e.g. special needs), or the whole staff through training days and other forms of in-service training.

The purposes of these activities are threefold:

- to involve staff as a whole in the process of reviewing the effectiveness and appropriateness of current procedures and practices within the school for identifying, recording and responding to pupils' learning needs and difficulties;

- to explore teachers' taken-for-granted assumptions about pupils' needs and abilities;

- to encourage a widespread sense of involvement in and 'ownership' of the whole process of initiating and implementing change and consolidating and building on existing good practices within the school.

'Differentiation in practice'

This is a whole staff activity intended partly to raise awareness of the issue of differentiation and to initiate the process of reviewing how the school currently provides for the differentiated learning needs and problems of individual pupils, particularly those labelled as 'low attainers', 'the less able', 'the underachievers'.

Activity 1:

(1) staff should be in small inter-departmental working groups (6-8);

(2) distribute copies of Diagram 1 (on page 10) to each group;

(3) ask groups to 'locate' on this Diagram:

- ❏ the school
- ❏ their respective departments
- ❏ their respective year teams;

(4) allow 15-20 minutes for group work and 15-20 minutes for whole staff review of what emerges from this activity;

(5) designate a member of staff with a whole school remit, e.g. head or co-ordinator of special needs, RoA co-ordinator, TVEI co-ordinator, etc.) to provide a summary of the discussions for circulation.

'Pupil portraits'

This is also a whole staff activity. The purpose is to stimulate discussion about the criteria currently being used in the school to identify pupils' learning needs and difficulties.

Activity 2:

Phase 1:

(1) circulate copies of the pupil portraits on pages 12-17;

(2) staff should be in small inter-departmental working groups;

(3) each group should then split into pairs with each pair selecting two pupils they are both teaching or have recently taught, who they would classify as 'lower attainers', 'less able', 'below average', 'underachievers', 'de-motivated' or just in need of specific help with certain learning tasks. Each pair of teachers should then be asked to produce 'pen portraits' on similar lines to those distributed; (no longer than 15 minutes);

(4) each pair of teachers should then identify where the school may not be fully meeting these pupils' needs and make specific recommendations about what ought to be done.

Phase 2:

(1) the pairs should then rejoin their inter-departmental groups and pool their pupil portraits;

(2) then distribute copies of the checklist on page 13 and ask each group to examine their pupil portraits in the light of this checklist to see which of these characteristics seem most applicable to each of the pupils they have selected;

(3) each group should then consider the recommendations made by each pair and attempt to draw up a more comprehensive set of proposals;

(4) during this activity put Diagram 2 (on page 14) on an overhead projector as an aid to discussion of the kinds of assumptions about pupils which have emerged during the activity to see how widespread such assumptions might be within the staff.

NOTE TO PLANNERS: The main aim of this activity is to encourage staff to explore and challenge their own and others' assumptions about pupils. Allow at least 40 minutes.

Activity 3:

'Testing the system'

The purpose of this activity is, as its title suggests, to test the existing system for collecting, recording and using information about pupils' learning needs and problems:

(1) At the end of Activity 2 each inter-departmental group should be asked to nominate one pupil in each year group (with either specific or general attainment and learning problems);

(2) Heads of year should then be asked to collect all available information on these pupils which appears germane to their learning difficulties and, using copies of the blank form on page 25 produce learning profiles for each pupil selected;

(3) Having completed these profiles, heads of year should then be asked to complete a short pro forma which asks the following questions:

- How long did the exercise take?

- Where was the information stored?

- In what form(s) was it available?

- Were there any major differences between departments/year tutors in the kind and quality of information provided?

- What gaps were there in the information available?

- How effective is the overall system for recording and retrieving information on pupils?

- What recommendations, if any, would they make for improving the system?

'Identifying pupils' learning needs'

Activity 4:

(1) Once the heads of year have collected information on the selected pupils and completed the learning profiles on them, these should be distributed to the inter-departmental working groups which had nominated those pupils;

(2) Each working group should then review the profiles in the light of their own experience of teaching them to see to what extent each profile adequately 'characterises' each pupil's learning needs and difficulties;

(3) Once each working group has been fully 'immersed' in the process of identifying learning needs, distribute copies of Box 1 and ask them to discuss how widespread they believe each type of lower attainment is within each year group in the school;

(4) Collect the estimates from each working group and review them with heads of year and the special needs co-ordinator and produce a summary for circulation. This could form the basis for future discussions of what needs to be done.

'Reviewing current practice'

So far these staff development activities have encouraged the whole staff to scrutinise (a) the assumptions which they make about pupils' attainment, performance and ability, and (b) the school's procedures for collecting, storing, retrieving and using information on pupils. Activity 5 takes this process a stage further and involves the whole staff in reviewing how the school currently responds to the diversity of learning needs which have been estimated in Activity 4.

Phase 1:

(1) Staff working in inter-departmental groups should critically review how the school currently responds to the different types of learning problems specified in Box 1 (on page 23) in terms of:

❏ SEN provision

❏ assessment and recording procedures

❏ curriculum provision

❏ classroom practices

❏ school organisation (including how the role of SEN co-ordinator is perceived and utilised)

❏ pastoral care;

(2) Each group should be asked to draw up a list identifying:

❏ good practices within their departments

❏ areas for improvement.

'Priorities for change'

At this point in the staff development process the whole staff have been encouraged to review existing procedures and practices from three distinct perspectives:

❏ as members of inter-departmental working groups

❏ as members of departmental teams

❏ as designated co-ordinators.

They have already been encouraged to identify the scope for improvement whilst wearing 'two hats'. The object of Activity 6 is to take this process a stage further and encourage them - working in inter-departmental or cross-curricular groups - to look at the good practices which have been identified and the recommendations for improvement which emerged from Activity 5 and assess each recommendation in terms of its pros and cons (along similar lines to Section 3) and on this basis draw up a set of general recommendations for the whole school:

❑ suggesting how the school can continue to support and build on existing good practices

❑ suggesting priorities for change, including how to spread good practice more easily.

'Logistics and practical realities'

Activity 7:

Activities 1-6 should have helped to initiate a process of consultation, participation and negotiation involving all the staff, but it is important at this stage to start to build the foundation for a realistic programme of change which is both feasible and will have widespread support amongst staff.

The school's management team should, therefore, take the recommendations which have emerged from the whole staff activities and:

- draw up an overall list of priorities for change which would command widespread support;

- distinguish between short-term changes and long-term changes;

- identify the likely organisational implications (e.g. staffing, timetabling, curriculum, resourcing, etc.) of such changes;

- list the likely constraints and problems that might hinder specific changes. In this respect it might be useful to draw up a list similar to the one which appears on page 26 of the Handbook. It is important to try to distinguish between:

INTERNAL FACTORS which could be overcome if there is the will to do so within the school;
EXTERNAL FACTORS which could be circumvented by changes in the organisation of the school, resource allocation, curriculum or classroom practices;
EXTERNAL FACTORS which are beyond the control of the school and must therefore be taken into account in any decisions taken.

Estimate the potential impact of the changes proposed and plan how best to cope with them. This kind of discussion might be assisted by distributing copies of some of the case study material in the Handbook.

AGENDA FOR LEAS: THE CHALLENGE OF 'LOW ATTAINMENT'

The aim here is to move out from the school to the LEA, and to ask, in the light of issues highlighted earlier, what role LEAs might have in encouraging the development of a whole school strategy for effective learning.

Here we face a difficulty: the relationship between LEAs and schools has undergone a major change over the last few years, but more particularly since the Education Reform Act and the introduction of local management. It is essential to bear these continuing changes in mind in drawing on our case study evidence. At the same time, the statutory role of the LEA in supporting and monitoring school improvement and in implementing and managing government-funded initiatives suggests that it is important to think about how LEA teams can foster school-based development of the kind envisaged in this Handbook.

This section begins by introducing the concepts of **integration** and **sponsorship** in relation to limited-term initiatives. It then discusses how some LEAs began to use the expertise of their project teams in a more broadly based strategy for 'raising attainment'. Lastly, some possible options for a longer-term LEA strategy for supporting schools are considered.

THINKING ABOUT MANAGING CHANGE THROUGH PROJECTS

Funded projects make special demands on educational managers who carry the responsibility for their success. A project requires continuing commitment from those responsible for it - in this case both national government and the LEA as the accountable body - if it is not to founder under the pressure of other more immediate priorities. This commitment has two complementary strands which usually differ in relative strength at various stages in the life of a project: **integration** and **sponsorship.**

> **Integration.** Refers to the effort made by the LEA to incorporate the project within a coherent overall strategy. Here the emphasis is on permeability between the project and other developments. The concept is relevant at all stages of the project's life. What was the rationale for taking the project on in the first place? Did it fit into a longer-term strategy? In planning the structure of the project, has the need to keep it within the mainstream concern of education officers and advisers been taken into account? How can the project, once it has been allowed to develop its own identity, be kept in step with LEA policy-making as a whole and with other related initiatives? How is constructive interaction between initiatives best achieved?

Sponsorship. Refers to the investment and protection afforded by the LEA to the project, marking it out for the duration of its extra funding as 'special'. This usually involves creating and maintaining a psychological barrier around the project, behind which project staff can feel free to experiment, but the form of sponsorship will vary markedly according to the character of the project. Planning an LEA project has to involve the creation of viable and appropriate structures and procedures for its implementation, and the definition of their relationship to the LEA as sponsoring body. Again the 'sponsorship' covers the whole life cycle of the innovation, including the transition of schemes in pilot schools to free-standing existence as funds are transferred elsewhere and the extension of the innovation to other schools.

The pattern of integration and sponsorship will be influenced by the form of the project and the context in which it operates. Most projects, however, follow a pattern in which sponsorship plays a stronger part in the early phases of initiation and implementation, with strategies for integration becoming more evident and relevant once it is firmly established and the potential for constructive links and exchanges with other developments becomes clearer. But thinking about integration needs to be built in from the first - indeed preferably the project will have grown out of existing policy - and sponsorship may have to outlive the period of external funding if the project is to bear good fruit. Some may collapse without the additional boost to running costs; those which entail fundamental changes in pedagogy are likely to fade unless there is a continuing framework of professional support for induction and review.

The concept of integration, in relation to curriculum projects, implies an LEA commitment to, and capacity for, strategic thinking about the curriculum. While this may now be generally taken for granted, it is in fact only since 1987 that all LEAs have been required to have an explicit curriculum policy to which new projects needed to be related. Integration can take many organisational forms from formal shared management structures to informal networks among teams or groups with overlapping interests. Whether or not a project which has been fully integrated into the LEA's own structure and programmes should retain its own identity is debatable and depends on the context. In the view of one Chief Education Officer: 'a project is successful when nobody knows it exists any more but we can see the water's risen by one or two inches'.

Sponsorship and integration in LAPP

The LAPP projects were all, in principle, LEA projects designed initially by LEA staff and initially led by LEA teams who provided support and, in some cases, controlled resources. The LEA, in most cases, continued to be an active sponsor of school-based initiatives. This was a challenging task. Different approaches were required in keeping with the type of 'solution' favoured by the project design. In one form or another, sponsorship involved:

- **provision of expertise:** skills specific to the project focus and expertise in managing change have both been essential;

- **resourcing:** effective sponsorship showed itself in the flexible and well monitored management of resources, responding creatively to schools' developing needs;

- **training and development:** long-term support was needed for teachers, particularly within their own school setting, to enable them to effect lasting change in classroom practice through the project experience;

- **evaluation and review:** it has proved difficult to develop procedures for securing constructively critical and timely evaluation advice within LEAs;

- **promotion:** a regular circulation of project newsletters and reports proved one effective strategy for raising awareness about the initiative.

Whether or not a project started out as or became an integrated element of LEA policy seemed to depend centrally on:

- **project direction,** formal and/or executive;

- the structure of **reporting and accountability;**

- the LEA stance on **strategic planning.**

Project direction

The strongest position, in terms of integration within overall LEA policy, was held by projects where from the start the project leaders had ready access to policy-makers at the highest level within the LEA. An assured position of this kind made it easier to recover from false starts and blind alleys and to retain an influence on events. It was much more difficult if the leadership was inappropriately located in the system (e.g. with FE rather than schools' advisory staff or under an adviser whose main work lay outside mainstream curriculum development) or if there was a major gap in status and function between those holding formal project responsibility and those providing day-to-day support to schools.

Reporting and accountability

An associated issue was the effectiveness of the monitoring and review system required for the project. Formally, all projects were expected by the DES to set up an LEA steering committee of some kind. What seemed to be needed, in addition to any formal monitoring system, was a regular forum in which project issues and insights could be effectively aired and evaluated with LEA policy-makers.

In this way obstacles to integration could be removed and promising project ideas identified and put forward for wider application. Without such a forum, it has proved difficult to publicise and disseminate solutions or strategies developed by individual schools, however apparently valuable.

LEAs' strategic planning

In at least one LEA, the LAPP project proved the catalyst for a new era in curriculum policy-making; it was not only integral to it, but became the starting point for other developments. More often, LEAs were developing strategic planning for the curriculum only after their LAPP project was initiated. It was then possible for the significance of the project within LEA policy to grow once there were demonstrable signs of success. Other LEAs found that the project did not fit well into their plan as circumstances changed.

SPONSORING LONG-TERM CHANGE THROUGH LAPP

Because the problems of 'lower attainment' have such deep roots, and because there are so many obstacles to comprehensive reappraisal of the issues, little progress is likely without continuing challenge and encouragement over a prolonged period. This is as true for schools as it is for individual teachers or students; it therefore has important implications for LEA 'change agents' who have the task of encouraging the school improvement process: project leaders, advisers and advisory teachers.

The impact of LAPP in this respect relates closely to the use which LEAs were able to make of the LEA project team. Whatever specific solutions were favoured by each LEA, LAPP funding has generated a considerable amount of learning (some of it unduly laborious and painful) about the effective management of change in the LEA and in schools. In this role the team came to act more as a catalyst in order to encourage schools to examine their practice, define the obstacles to improving achievement and select an appropriate mix and timetable of remedial measures, than as a provider of solutions. Keeping a LAPP team together was one way of conserving this hard-won expertise and has proved to be one of the additional and perhaps unintended returns on the LAPP investment, demonstrating the benefits of building strong and resilient teams in order to support initiatives which question conventional wisdom and practice.

There has been a remarkable degree of continuity in project leadership over the whole period of LAPP (1983-89) in over half the 17 projects. The value of the experience and expertise that has accrued is recognised by at least seven LEAs which have invested their own funds in keeping teams together and providing new contracts or by incorporating the team members into the permanent structure of LEA advisory staff. But continuity, valuable though it can be in enabling team members to develop the necessary skills of supporting and managing change, is not enough. Two other ingredients, identified as important for the pilot phase of the initiative, seem to be increasingly significant if an LEA team is to play a continuing role in challenging more schools to consider how they can raise attainment:

Access to policy-makers not only within the LEA (a point to which we will return) but also in schools. However successful LEA project leaders and team members are with teachers and in classrooms, LAPP experience suggests that their influence and the influence of the initiative in raising questions about 'attainment' for the school as a whole will be limited unless their work is embedded within the plans and the thinking of the senior management team.

Practical expertise with a sound theoretical foundation. As we have seen, LAPP initiatives have identified differing aspects of attainment as their way into the longer-term task of reshaping teacher and learner attitudes and the effectiveness of classroom practice. The common element is expertise in making change happen: a combination of recognised INSET skills and a range of other strengths such as: tutoring, evaluating, demonstrating, challenging and negotiating. The distinctive element is the particular area of pedagogy in which each team has specialised: in oracy, thinking skills, assessment and recording, curriculum design and the preparation of differentiated materials and so on. Where it has been possible to draw on and continue to strengthen a solid professional underpinning for the chosen approach, teachers have been quick to recognise the value of what the team can offer.

The problem about sponsoring attainment reviews in schools is that, if they are to be effective, they very quickly have to break out of the kind of framework that LAPP set up. LEA teams working on strategies closely tied to the 14-16 framework, for example alternative accreditation schemes, have in this respect been limited in developing their work within secondary schools, although special schools have seen the potential of new forms of curriculum and assessment for pupils of varying ages and stages. By contrast, teams working on Thinking Skills schemes have more readily chosen to work with younger secondary pupils. This suggests a third factor to be taken into account in sponsoring a 'lower attainers' team as agents for an action programme on attainment:

Expertise relevant to all teachers and pupils, not too inextricably identified with the 14-16 'lower attainers' context.

Integrating LAPP into an LEA action programme on attainment: two examples

Whether or not the LAPP team had worked on its own hitherto, a decision to sponsor the team for a long-term role, with a broader remit in raising attainment, quickly raised questions about how such work fitted in with that of other regular support groups - particularly subject advisers and special needs support staff - and of major initiatives such as TVEI and RoAs. In some LAPP LEAs, indeed, it was not thought appropriate or cost-effective to maintain the LAPP team when the external funding was phased out. Instead, key LAPP personnel have been placed in charge of other initiatives or have acquired posts in the advisory service, thus retaining their expertise within the central curriculum planning team while dissolving the LAPP identity. In at least two LEAs, the project was an integral part of LEA planning from the outset, and LAPP leaders have been able to move into a broader 'school improvement' role within the context of the Education Reform Act and its demands. In another two there has been an explicit decision to develop a 'raising attainment' initiative with a broader remit than LAPP, using LAPP personnel and building on LAPP expertise and ideas. The two examples differ in their scope and in the way in which the LEA has integrated the initiative (a) with other projects and (b) with its overall policy and permanent structures (advisers, officers and so on).

In this LEA the LAPP initiative spawned two locally funded projects: one was developing a Thinking Skills programme and the other had a broad 'raising attainment' remit.This was in keeping with a tradition that had grown up in the LEA of backing many projects and encouraging creative enterprise, while leaving future directions and relationships open. Each project had its own small central team whose members had all come from some branch of the LEA's LAPP project, and these teams operated independently from each other and, in an organisational sense, from other LEA structures (apart from formal accountability to LEA senior management). Our interest here is in the 'raising attainment' project, which as the direct descendent of the LEA's LAPP initiative, retained the same project leader who indeed ran the new project and the dissemination phase of the old project in tandem. The team fully acknowledge that they had learned from LAPP and indeed used that experience in the formulation of the new project. At the end of the first term the aims of the new project could be expressed thus:

Example 1:

- *to ensure that there is a clear focus on the issues of underachievement in the authority*

in order to

- *improve the achievement and attainment of pupils who may not be reaching their full potential at school;*

- *broaden the criteria by which success is measured in schools;*

- *extend the range of contexts for learning offered to pupils;*

- *improve motivation, involvement, self-esteem and confidence in pupils.*

Three of the four schools involved were formerly 'outer ring' schools in LAPP. All four were offered additional resources in the form of a seconded 'change agent' who acted as a link between two of the schools and the centre. There were also internal secondments in each school and some pump-priming cash. It was up to each school to pin-point areas of work and issues about achievement that they wished to explore within the project framework, but all were encouraged to investigate patterns of underachievement. By dint of frequent meetings and visits, the central team have been able to build the trust that is needed to encourage and stimulate real questioning about how the school thinks about attainment. Even though the life of the new project in any one school is limited to two years, it has been possible to use inter-school networks and meetings, particularly through the work of the internal school secondees, to enable the school to learn quickly. In practice, a family of investigations and curriculum developments has taken place during the first year of the scheme, with many overlaps among schools. For the second year, new school enrolments include two 'families' of secondary schools with feeder primary schools, creating opportunities to explore the issue of progression across the primary-secondary divide.

In funding this (as well as the Thinking Skills programme) the LEA has maintained its tradition of sponsorship for innovative projects, but only recently has the issue of integration been fully addressed. There was a risk that the 'raising attainment' project, small in scale, physically isolated from TVEI, RoAs and other initiatives which were housed in a separate development centre and with no direct access to LEA policy groups, would be marginalised as a rump of the earlier lower attainers initiative. In practice close links have been forged with a team working on unit accreditation, and there has been some interchange with other initiatives, although it is usually the smaller project that has made the running. A new commitment to include the project leader on equal terms with other LEA senior staff in regular planning meetings has recently brought the project into the centre of LEA thinking. At the same time, there is a continuing tension between the close and effective relationships that can be developed relatively quickly by working with a few schools and the intention to spread the messages of the project through the LEA.

Another LEA which had a much more unitary LAPP project than the previous one, focusing on a common pattern of 'alternative curriculum' activities in all eight pilot schools, took a considered decision to redirect the initiative for the dissemination phase and after. The transition here has carried central funding over into this phase with the LEA committing itself to a continuing programme with an increasing share of local funding up to the end of the funded period. Both sponsorship and integration were on the agenda in the new plan. It was decided to exploit the TVEI framework of local consortia of schools as the organisational base for the 'raising attainment' project now building on

Example 2:

the momentum of a major curriculum initiative. Here too there was some continuity of personnel, although the team was built on a secondment basis, and it was therefore unlikely that, apart from the project leader, any one member would remain in post for more than one or two years. The central focus of the new project is on differentiation. This is seen as a way of providing a more effective education by tailoring methods and materials to the needs of individuals and monitoring their progress systematically. However, the transition also involved a shift of focus away from directly supporting pupils and towards supporting teachers in developing their work with pupils across the age range 11-16. The method the project has chosen is to respond to schools' expressed needs, particularly within the four TVEI consortia to which the four advisory teachers in the project team were attached during the first year of the new scheme. The agenda for their work with the schools is informed by the project guidelines on differentiation, but in fact is broad and non-specific.

Over the first year of the new initiative, much exciting work has been done by the team in helping teachers in the project schools to develop 'differentiated' materials and to assist with profiling. But there are concerns that their efforts may be spread too thinly and lack the impetus that comes from whole school commitment to the project. For this reason there are plans to strengthen this commitment through school project 'contracts'. The position of the advisory teachers in relation to school senior managers depends heavily on goodwill, and they only have the one year to consolidate it. The link with TVEI has in some respects proved less relevant than had been hoped as schools respond to the new project in the light of the demands of the National Curriculum. However, since the project has two more years to develop, and it has the wholehearted commitment of senior staff in the LEA and the Education Committee, it has the opportunity to make a significant contribution to LEA practice in raising attainment as a whole.

The two examples illustrate differing approaches to the same broad strategy of using a small central team to work with schools on raising attainment.

Example 1:

> *small number of schools* - maximum impact by team on each
> *broad agenda* - within which to negotiate 'attainment' focus
> *school senior management involvement* - as part of contract
> *internal secondments* - plus external support for school

Example 2:

> *large number of schools* - to increase coverage
> *single theme (differentiation)* - to provide a clear focus
> *direct work with classroom teachers* - to enhance credibility
> *collaboration on 'products'* - can be used by other schools

Moreover, although each represents a significant local investment, they occupy different places within the LEA scheme of things. In example one, links with other initiatives are personal rather than structured, but the project leader is now a member of a central LEA planning team. The project staff (with strong LAPP roots) have two or three year contracts, which provide continuity. In example two, the project was initially set within a TVEI framework, but the two have less in common than perhaps was originally envisaged. A strong link has now developed with the LEA special needs team, suggesting that the process of integration needs to take account of overlapping interest groups at LEA level, all of which are concerned in some way with the theme of differentiation and raising attainment. Continuity is encouraged by early identification of next year's team members, and expertise is disseminated as secondees return to schools. Each project has yet to be fully integrated within a coherent, fully integrated LEA strategy for school improvement in relation to attainment.

LONGER TERM BENEFITS: TOWARDS AN INTEGRATED STRATEGY FOR RAISING ATTAINMENT

In the period since 1987, covering the major part of the LAPP 'transition' phase, the passing of the Education Reform Act has transformed the climate for discussing educational performance of all kinds. Multiple demands for change both require and, in practical terms, often impede the forging of coherent, integrated strategies because of the scale of the requirements and the speed with which they are introduced.

Even before 1988, the introduction of GCSE had demonstrated the need that all schools had for coherent LEA in-service programmes on assessment, differentiation and other attainment-related themes. As LEA officers and head teachers are only too aware, this pressure is now growing. Thus the National Curriculum and assessment programme is giving a new urgency and definition to many of the attainment-related issues that have arisen in LAPP. At the same time, pressure to reshape roles at LEA level, and the need to justify all LEA-funded posts, constrains plans for building any new central teams. In the present context of what is now being called innovation overload, will it be possible to construct an integrated strategy to meet these demands, and what indications are there from LAPP of the strengths and weaknesses of the various routes towards this goal?

It had already become clear before the Act that the **integration of funded initiatives** within a single framework (which has happened to some extent in a few LAPP LEAs) was one way of working towards a single or coherent long-term LEA strategy that could accommodate further change. Alternatively, placing project staff, such as LAPP team leaders who had made 'raising attainment' issues a priority, within **integrated LEA development teams** has proved a feasible and potentially powerful way of building a 'raising attainment' policy.

Increasingly, however, it is the **impetus of statutory change** which matters and, as was suggested earlier, there is now a pressing need to exploit any available expertise in order to construct an LEA strategy for enabling schools to make the most of every pupil's potential over the whole 5-16 period. The LAPP experience has underlined some of the priorities that have to be recognised before a strategy can become effective. For example:

- the entitlement of every pupil to high levels of attainment (not the lowering of expectations for some);

- the need to recognise the diversity of needs among pupils, among schools and, over time, for individuals;

- the importance of both diagnosing and following up learning problems.

As has been suggested in earlier sections, it could be that the prime curricular contribution to be made by developers to an integrated action programme on attainment is to work at implementing much needed **pedagogical solutions** (differentiated learning approaches to common learning targets) for what have hitherto often been seen as **organisational problems** (getting the right children into groups for the right type or level of course). This would probably involve co-operation with special needs staff and RoA teams being maintained by many LEAs even without the statutory endorsement many had anticipated, as well as with other groups developing aspects such as oracy or problem-solving. Staff from LAPP teams have expressed anxiety about the threat which they considered current Key Stage 4 assessment and accreditation proposals pose to curriculum opportunities for some 14-16 pupils. The broader challenge for LEAs is how to maximise available expertise in helping teachers to develop effective pedagogical solutions for the whole secondary age and ability range.

At the same time, there is also the task of securing appropriate conditions within schools for pedagogical solutions to take effect. Increasingly, this may mean using knowledge gained from working through 'raising attainment' programmes in schools in order to contribute to effective resource planning and the monitoring of school development programmes. From LAPP national and local evaluations and the experience of those working with 'lower attainers' at school and LEA level, there is valuable evidence of pitfalls to be avoided as well as more effective tactics for enabling schools to embark on their own long-term programme. For example, there is the importance of recognising the many differences between schools and how these influence thinking about attainment. An LEA action programme would need to accommodate these differences, but also to ask, as the various elements of the Act take effect, whether any schools are facing conditions which preclude the kind of review and reform strategy which has been envisaged here.

The problem of overload (too many projects, too many pressures) can now be guaranteed to strike a chord at any gathering of educational professionals. Issues of **differentiation, progression, coherence** and **motivation** that are central to the effective implementation of the National Curriculum have been at the heart of LAPP work, and are being explicitly addressed in a number of LEAs in the LAPP follow-up. Hard-won insight into and experience of how to enable teachers and schools to work through the changes in pedagogy that are implied must not be wasted.

References

Better Schools: Evaluation and Appraisal Conference DES 1986

A View of the Curriculum, HMI HMSO 1980

Committee of Inquiry into the Education of Handicapped Children and Young People **(The Warnock Report)** DES, 1978 Special Educational Needs

NFER Reports on the Lower Attainment Pupils Programme

1. *The Search for Success:* an overview of the Programme 1983-6

2. *Relationships for Learning:* building trust and raising expectations

3. *Practical Learning:* the challenge to pupils and teachers

4. *Learning to Learn:* helping pupils to improve their educational competence

5. *Purposeful Learning:* assessment and progression

6. *Frameworks for Learning:* pupils' projects and the structure of the curriculum

7. *Professional Practice:* implications for teacher development and support

8. *Budgeting for Change:* implications for the resourcing of curriculum initiatives

9. *Residentials:* as a resource for learning

Printed in the United Kingdom for HMSO
Dd 293364 3/91 C40 488 20249